FROM THE BRONX TO WALL STREET

"Think of giving not only as a duty but as a privilege."

— JOHN D. ROCKEFELLER

"If you're in the luckiest one percent of humanity, you owe it to the rest of humanity to think about the other ninety-nine percent."

— WARREN BUFFETT

"The three most powerful things in business: a kind word, a thoughtful gesture, and passion and enthusiasm for everything you're doing."

— KEN LANGONE

"I think you have a moral responsibility when you've been given far more than you need, to do wise things with it and give intelligently."

— J. K. ROWLING

"Surplus wealth is a sacred trust which its possessor is bound to administer in his lifetime for the good of the community."

— ANDREW CARNEGIE

"What you do for yourself dies with you when you leave this world; what you do for others, lives on forever."

— KEN ROBINSON

FROM THE BRONX TO WALL STREET

MY FIFTY YEARS IN
FINANCE AND PHILANTHROPY

LEON COOPERMAN

 Advantage | Books

Published by Advantage, Charleston, South Carolina.
Member of Advantage Media.

ADVANTAGE is a registered trademark, and the Advantage colophon is a trademark of Advantage Media Group, Inc.

Printed in the United States of America.

10 9 8 7 6 5 4 3 2 1

ISBN: 978-1-64225-622-2 (Hardcover)

LCCN: 2023904263

Cover design by Matthew Morse.
Layout design by Matthew Morse.

This publication is designed to provide accurate and authoritative information in regard to the subject matter covered. It is sold with the understanding that the publisher is not engaged in rendering legal, accounting, or other professional services. If legal advice or other expert assistance is required, the services of a competent professional person should be sought.

Advantage Media helps busy entrepreneurs, CEOs, and leaders write and publish a book to grow their business and become the authority in their field. Advantage authors comprise an exclusive community of industry professionals, idea-makers, and thought leaders. Do you have a book idea or manuscript for consideration? We would love to hear from you at **AdvantageMedia.com**.

This book is dedicated to my family.

CONTENTS

INTRODUCTION

The purpose of life is to discover your gift. The work of life is to develop it. The meaning of life is to give your gift away.

— DAVID VISCOTT, AMERICAN PSYCHIATRIST

We all have special gifts, passions, and missions. Some of us are here to compose beautiful music, design great buildings, heal the sick, master an Olympic sport, or teach in a way that excites young minds and inspires them to excellence.

Following a childhood growing up in the rough-and-tumble South Bronx, I was in my early twenties when, after a false start in dental school, I discovered my own special gift and passion: an uncanny talent for understanding the intricacies of Wall Street finance. I spent my career developing that gift through hard work and perseverance and, in the process, made a lot of money.

Now, in my sunset years, I am engaged in giving my gift away — all of it, my entire fortune.

My goal in writing this memoir is to expand on some of the lessons I have learned while navigating the voyage of my life, to explain the inspiration and rationale for my philanthropy, and, in the course

1

of it all, to make the case for a robust economic system that, despite its manifold benefits, has recently found itself under siege — capitalism.

Under no other system would I, the son of a Polish immigrant plumber, have had the opportunity to rise to the position in which I am now blessed to find myself. The same goes for my good friend Ken Langone, another son of a plumber and the cofounder of Home Depot. Writing in his autobiography, Ken notes that he himself is living proof that capitalism not only works, but that it can work for "anybody and everybody. Blacks and whites and browns and everyone in between.... Show me where the silver spoon was in my mouth ... I'm the American Dream."

Under no other system would I, the son of a Polish immigrant plumber, have had the opportunity to rise to the position in which I am now blessed to find myself.

So am I, as are many, many others — from Andrew Carnegie, the son of an impoverished Scottish handloom weaver who became a lion of the American steel industry during the Gilded Age, to my fellow Bronx veteran and close friend Mario Gabelli, the son of Italian immigrants, who has risen to the very top ranks of American finance.

Both of these men have been, in their time, very generous philanthropists and benefactors for the public good, as have General Motors' Charles Stewart Mott and Alfred P. Sloan, Berkshire Hathaway's Warren Buffett, and Microsoft's Bill and Melinda Gates, to name just a few.

It was Carnegie who, in 1889, wrote that "he who dies rich dies disgraced." To this, Carnegie added:

... the surplus which accrues from time to time in the hands of a man should be administered by him in his own lifetime for that purpose, which is seen by him, as trustee, to be best for the good of the people.... The gospel of wealth ... calls upon the millionaire to sell all that he hath and give it in the highest and best form to the poor by administering his estate himself for the good of his fellows, before he is called upon to lie down and rest upon the bosom of Mother Earth.

Carnegie, who did not believe in the notion of inherited wealth, gave away more than 90 percent of his $380 million fortune before his death in 1919, building over three thousand libraries and endowing or funding the Carnegie Corporation of New York, the Carnegie Foundation for the Advancement of Teaching, the Carnegie Endowment for International Peace, and the Tuskegee Institute (now Tuskegee University), among other philanthropic endeavors. Upon his death, the bulk of his remaining $30 million estate was further recycled into his charities, with a small remainder going to fund retirements for his personal staff.

Inspired by the examples of such people as Carnegie, I have begun the process of giving away the material fruits of my life's work. I have taken the Giving Pledge, originated by Bill and Melinda Gates and Warren Buffett, which obliges signatories to publicly undertake to donate at least half their wealth. But I have gone even further, promising the remainder of my wealth as well, just as Warren himself has pledged 99 percent of his own. I have also taken the Jewish Future Pledge with my friend Mike Leven, which seeks to ensure that vibrant Jewish life continues for generations to come by calling upon subscribers to pledge half or more of the charitable giving in their estate plans to support the Jewish people and/or the State of Israel.

In the pages that follow, you will find my reasons for doing this, along with a firm defense of the economic system that has enabled me and many others, including those mentioned above, to build the fortunes we did and are now privileged to dedicate to the public good. These include visionary entrepreneurs and financiers involved in the founding, funding, and facilitating of vital enterprises, which have become successful by supplying necessary goods and services, not to mention jobs, that have greatly benefited society and who have themselves thereby prospered while bringing prosperity to others.

As I approach my eightieth birthday, I recall the words of legendary Yankee first baseman Lou Gehrig, who on July 4, 1939, uttered these famous words at a home-plate ceremony at Yankee Stadium: "For the past two weeks, you have been reading about a bad break. Yet today I consider myself the luckiest man on the face of the earth." Thirty-six at the time, he died two years later at thirty-eight.

While I have had some setbacks along the way, I am truly one of the lucky ones, not only in business but, more importantly, in family. I met my wife, Toby, in 1962 in a French class at Hunter College, and she became my life partner upon graduation in 1964. She has been an integral part of my success. Together, we raised two outstanding sons who, while very different, have achieved great success in their respective fields: our oldest, Wayne, a Phi Beta Kappa graduate of Stanford University with an MBA from the University of Pennsylvania's Wharton School, became an accomplished money manager; his younger brother, Michael, with an undergraduate degree from Tufts, a Master's Degree from the University of Montana and a Ph.D. from Oregon State University, is a fisheries scientist focusing on the environment. When people ask me what I consider to be my greatest accomplishments, I think of my kids and of how proud I am that they still come home and that we have excellent relationships.

Both sons enlarged our immediate family by marrying wives – Jodi and Anne – who are very special in their own right. Those marriages have produced three spectacular grandchildren: Courtney, twenty-five; Kyra, twenty-two; and Asher, fourteen. My grandchildren have been raised by excellent parents and are all sensible, engaged citizens.

In the end, my principal ambition in writing this volume is to leave a bit of myself behind for these and future generations of my family whom I will never meet, so that they might understand what I experienced and learned in the course of my life, along with my philosophy — what I have come to believe, including about the merits of capitalism and the importance of being a capitalist with a heart, and how I've arrived at those beliefs. This book is both dedicated to them and is my loving legacy to them.

I want to thank my longtime colleague, partner and friend, David Bloom, and my publishing consultant and more recent friend, Edward Renehan, for their great work in helping me write this book. It has been a pleasure.

Leon Cooperman
Boca Raton, Florida
February 2023

PART I

FORMATIVE YEARS

CHAPTER 1

FIRST GENERATION

Teachers open the door, but you must enter by yourself.

— CHINESE PROVERB

My roots are humble and, to a large extent, obscure. My father, Harry Cooperman, came to the United States from Poland in 1920, at age twelve, and started working as a plumber's apprentice. His father (my grandfather, Isidor), whom I knew well as a youngster, was a barrel-maker by trade, albeit a very bookish one who spent a lot of time with my father's sister at the local library near where the family lived, on Simpson Street in The Bronx — the Forty-first Precinct, more notoriously known as "Fort Apache."

Of the Cooperman family's place of origin in Poland, I have no idea, although I seem to recall my father or grandfather saying that in Poland the name had actually been *Cooperwasa*. All in all, I am woefully ignorant of every aspect of my family's history before their arrival in the United States. This goes as well for my mother Martha's family, the Rothensteins, she also being a Polish émigré. I wish I knew more. In fact, I can't honestly say whether my parents knew each other in Poland or met in the United States. I do know, however, that they were married here in the States in February 1935.

I was born in The Bronx on April 25, 1943, when my mother was thirty-six and my father was thirty-five. I had one brother, Howard, seven years my senior, who passed away last year. There was another brother between the two of us who died before I came on the scene. In fact, he died of pneumonia in the backseat of my father's car while my parents were rushing him to the hospital. If he'd survived, perhaps I would have never been born. I can't say for sure.

Neither of my parents had much formal education, but both were smart people. My father read *The New York Times* every day. Professionally, he worked extremely hard as an independent plumber, putting in long days in order to support his family. I can't remember him ever taking a vacation. He had relationships with many landlords all around The Bronx and was regularly on call to solve all sorts of problems and address all kinds of emergencies on a moment's notice. Keep in mind that none of these buildings, mostly tenements, had elevators. So in addition to doing the plumbing work, my father was often hauling sinks, toilets, piping, and other heavy items up narrow staircases to ninth or tenth floors. In fact, when he was only seventy-one (relatively young, certainly by today's standards) and had retired to Florida due to a heart condition, he died of a heart attack while doing a favor for a friend, carrying a sink he was going to install up a flight of stairs. He was always very generous in that way, willing to help anyone with anything. That was a great quality of his, one of many.

My father's prodigious work ethic by no means made him a rich man. I would say that we were lower middle-class and that my parents were very frugal. The tenement apartment in which I spent most of my childhood had one bedroom. Our clothes always got patched before they got replaced. We never went to restaurants. The only luxurious "evening out" that I remember was once going to Radio City Music Hall to see Esther Williams in the 1952 film *Million Dollar Mermaid*. But that splurge was never repeated.

Given all this, it will come as no surprise to learn that I worked all sorts of jobs as a kid. I remember changing tires and fixing flats at Johnny's Tire Shop on Aldus Street. I bagged fruit at a fruit market. My first serious job, however (when I received a W-2), was as an usher at the Loew's Paradise Theater on the Grand Concourse in The Bronx, earning fifty or maybe fifty-five cents an hour. I remember seeing Cecil B. DeMille's *The Ten Commandments* (which came out in 1956, when I was thirteen) so many times that I almost had it memorized. I also worked a number of summers as a waiter and busboy in the Borscht Belt.

My father always encouraged me when it came to work. The one time he became displeased was when I was perhaps twelve. I'd gotten myself a shoeshine box and had started shining shoes on the street corner at fifteen cents a pair. For some reason, he thought this was beneath me. When he found out what I was doing, he came and pulled me home by the scruff of the neck, thus ending my career as a would-be shoeshine mogul.

Of course, there was also time for play. We played stickball in the street, basketball at the nearby park, baseball, and football. We went swimming in the East River, jumping and diving off the piers. We didn't think about it being polluted. People didn't have that sensibility in the forties and fifties. Back then, there was raw sewage going directly into the river, along with industrial waste, chemicals, and oil – a real toxic soup, but we didn't care. We just wanted to swim for relief in the summer when the tenements and streets got unbearably hot and humid. Our ignorance was bliss.

I had four friends in particular with whom I always spent a lot of time — Steve Aschengrau, Mike Kaplan, Howard Danziger, and Irwin Rothschild. The five of us were inseparable and played lots of sports after school and on the weekends. Now they are all gone. Steve Aschengrau passed at forty from pancreatic cancer, Mike Kaplan at seventy from a heart attack, and Howard Danziger and Irwin Rothschild both at around seventy-two from cancer. Of the old crowd, I'm the only one left.

Believe it or not, in addition to swimming in the polluted river, we also fished in the river and brought the fish home and ate them. We'd get porgies, striped bass, bluefish, flounder (fluke), and blackfish. God only knows what contaminants were in them. I'm guessing we got somewhat healthier fish when we'd go out on the inexpensive fishing party boats that would take crowds up the East River and into Long Island Sound for a day, or sometimes for a night. But as with the water, we didn't think about pollution in the fish. The question was not on our radar. Those were very different times.

At least the fish were kosher. My parents were proud of their Jewishness, but it wasn't all-consuming. They spoke Yiddish at home. My father went to the synagogue when he could, but if he had a plumbing job to do on a Saturday morning, he'd do the plumbing and skip the *shul*. He needed the money. Both my brother and I were *bar mitzvah*ed when our times came, and the family observed Passover and other holidays. I would say that, today, I am somewhat less observant than my parents were, even though I've actively supported a great many Jewish charities (along with other charities associated with other faiths).

So far as politics went, my parents were great fans of Franklin D. Roosevelt, as were a lot of Jews at that time. We now know that FDR shared a lot of the bigotries of his class, including anti-Semitism. After all, he turned away the boatload of Jews who had escaped Nazi

Germany on the *St. Louis* in 1939, sending them back to their certain deaths. And a few years later, during World War II, he refused (on the advice of Joseph P. Kennedy and others in his Administration) to order the bombing of the railroads that everyone knew were busy transporting countless Jews, among others, to extermination camps. FDR's inaction was at best a sign of apathy and at worst of antipathy. But my parents knew nothing of that. And they weren't alone. I've read that FDR got over 80 percent of the Jewish vote in all four of his presidential elections. So it seems the attitude in my home was common in Jewish households generally.

The most important thing to my parents was education — that my brother Howard and I should pay attention to our studies and do our best so that we could advance ourselves in life and go further than my parents had been able to, given their backgrounds and circumstances. Despite all this encouragement, I was at first just an average student, neither a failure nor a kid with his name on the honor roll. I ran with the herd, even though I was blessed with some fine public schools. Call it *mazel* – the kind of *mazel* that has stuck with me through the years.

One of the earliest instances of my good fortune was the opportunity to study at a fine public grammar school, P.S. Seventy-five in Southeast Bronx. It's right on the Bruckner Expressway. I occasionally pass it when I drive up to Connecticut. I lived two blocks from the school, so I walked there. After that, I attended Morris High School in Southwest Bronx, where I received an

> Call it *mazel* – the kind of *mazel* that has stuck with me through the years.

excellent education.[1] This was in the Melrose area, at the intersection of Boston Road and 166th Street, not far from my house. The quality of the school is perhaps best reflected in the number of distinguished alumni it can boast. These include Bernard Botein, a presiding justice of the New York Supreme Court (Appellate Division) and a president of the New York City Bar Association; film critic Judith Crist; industrialist Armand Hammer; distinguished television journalist Gabe Pressman; Chairman of the Joint Chiefs of Staff, National Security Advisor, and US Secretary of State Colin Powell; and film directors Jules Dassin and Arthur Seidelman, to name just a few. In short, Morris High School was always a place that inspired ambition and where students were imbued with the ethic of diligent hard work as a key factor leading to success.

That certainly was my takeaway, one that has helped carry me from my very modest Bronx beginnings to billionaire status — a designation that doesn't mean that much to me as I'm intent on giving all my money away.

I should emphasize that Morris was a public school and that all my education through my bachelor's degree was at public schools. I particularly remember Morris as being a very democratic place. I mean that with a small "d". During the late fifties when I was a student there, over half the student body was Black, which was unusual back then. It was also the first coeducational high school in the city. I loved the school and its diversity. In 1958, when I was a junior, my family moved from South Bronx to North Bronx. At the time, I could have transferred to Roosevelt High School, which was within walking distance from our new residence at 197th Street and Marion Avenue,

---

1   As of 2002, the school has been renamed the Morris Educational Campus and embraces four small specialty high schools: School for Violin and Dance, Bronx International, the School for Excellence, and the Morris Academy for Collaborative Studies.

but I elected to stay at Morris. I commuted there every day on the Third Avenue El from Fordham Road.

The building always was, and still is, very beautiful. Looking at it, you'd never think of the place as an inner-city high school catering to a bunch of kids from modest backgrounds. It's very gothic, dates from 1904, and looks like something you'd normally find on an Ivy League college campus. Five stories. Buff brick decorated with limestone and terra cotta details. A turreted central tower. A vast, gabled, green copper roof and an eight-story entrance archway. Really something to behold. So beautiful, in fact, that it is now registered by New York City as the hub of the Morris High School Historic District and was placed on the National Register of Historic Places back in 1983.

But for me, it was where I found my launchpad into college — Hunter College, now called Lehman College — upon graduation in 1960.

CHAPTER 2

GOOD LUCK, HARD WORK, AND INTUITION

An investment in knowledge pays the best interest.

— BENJAMIN FRANKLIN

In 2014, my wife, Toby, and I were pleased to be able to gift $25 million to our alma mater, Hunter College. Jennifer Raab, Hunter College's president at the time, tells me this is the largest gift given to the school to date. Fifteen million of this gift is going to help support the Leon & Toby Cooperman Library, with the remainder earmarked to anchor a scholarship fund for gifted students with financial needs who have exhausted all other potential sources for financial aid. Toby and I met at Hunter, where we were both students at the school's Bronx campus – now called Lehman College and, like Hunter, a part of the City University of New York. At Hunter, Toby and I both received very good educations for the grand fee of $24 a semester. As evidenced by the size of our scholarship gift, the tuition has (as they say) "gone up," but what hasn't?

Hunter had a long tradition of serving the working class of New York City. When it opened in February 1870 as the Female Normal and High School, it was the first tuition-free teacher's college in the country. Not long after, the New York legislature changed the name to the Normal College of the City of New York. Finally, in 1914, it became Hunter College of the City of New York, named after the school's founding president, Thomas Hunter. As of 1917, the school offered evening classes for working people eager to advance themselves. Throughout its history, the school positioned itself to serve undergraduate students who — whether for reasons of finance, class, social standing, or (frankly) ethnicity — would not typically have been accepted into most private institutions of higher education, which tended in the early twentieth century to be bastions of the WASP (White Anglo-Saxon Protestant) elite.

When I arrived on campus in the autumn of 1960, the place reminded me very much of the high school that I'd just left, as the student population represented a wide mix of students of color and first-generation White Americans with parents from Central Europe and elsewhere. Nearly all of us represented the first generation in our families to attend college. The atmosphere was one of opportunity. It seems to me that we all felt rather lucky to be where we were, with the promise of good futures so long as we were willing to work hard and take responsibility for advancing ourselves. And that happened for a great many of us. The famed journalist Eleanor Clift graduated in 1961, three years ahead of Toby and me. Other graduates include the distinguished writer Grace Paley, politician Bella Abzug, Massachusetts Institute of Technology (MIT) physicist Mildred Dresselhaus, artist Robert Morris, economist Jared Bernstein, journalist Jack Newfield, attorney Martin Garbus, and famed film critic (and fellow Morris High School alum) Judith Crist.

The biggest, unexpected bonus of Hunter College for me was Toby. We were both from The Bronx, although we'd attended different high schools. Her father, Morris, was an immigrant from Romania, although her mother, Sylvia, had been born in the United States. Her father sold fabrics, and her mother worked as a bookkeeper. Toby impressed me from the start as being very smart, honest, hardworking, and beautiful. Although we'd been acquaintances through our freshman year at Hunter, we got to know each other well after we enrolled in the same sophomore French class, where Toby helped me a great deal. The language did not come as easily to me as it did to her. The following academic year (1962–1963), Toby served as president of our junior class, and I as vice president. As time went on, we became increasingly interested in each other. At the end of our junior year, as class officers, we had free tickets to the junior prom. She asked me to be her date. As I've said more than once before, the price was right. From then on, we were an item. She wore my fraternity pin, which was how things were done at the time. It was seen as something of a precursor to becoming engaged.

Toby's interest, and the focus of her studies, was education. She went on to have a long, successful career in special education, helping kids with learning disabilities, sometimes quite severe learning disabilities in neurologically impaired children and children suffering from birth defects. This turned out to be her calling, and she has remained devoted to it. For more than two decades, she worked at the Early Childhood Learning Center in Chatham, New Jersey, a school dedicated to helping special-education students. More recently, she established a special-needs department at the Leon and Toby Cooperman Jewish Community Center of MetroWest New Jersey. She has also served as a member of United Jewish Communities of MetroWest's ABLE Committee, a network of community leaders and trained professionals who collaborate to support and advocate for individuals with special needs and their families. And these are just the "tip of the iceberg" of her many efforts through the years.

During my first year at Hunter, I joined the Alpha Epsilon Pi (AEPi) fraternity, which is the world's largest Jewish college fraternity, with branches on numerous campuses nationwide. In 1962, I served as pledge master, and in 1963 I was elected president. During my time as pledge master and president, I worked hard (and successfully) to dramatically increase the number of members. We had a good-sized frat house, and there was a great deal of pleasure and camaraderie. I truly enjoyed the Greek life and made good friends, but I'm sorry to say that most of those connections were lost through the years. We all had lives to live and moved on to other things. I was nevertheless quite honored and humbled in 2016 to receive one of AEPi's highest honors, the Arthur and Simi Teich Award for Distinguished Alumni Achievement, presented at the 103rd International Convention of AEPi in Fort Lauderdale, Florida.

At the time that I met Toby, I was taking mostly science courses and thinking generally about a possible career in dentistry. My major was chemistry. During that period, if you had finished the requirements for your major in three years, Hunter allowed you to count your first year of medical or dental school toward your fourth year of college. With this in mind, I took an intensive course in physical chemistry at the University of Pennsylvania during the summer of 1963, thus completing the requirements for my Hunter major. That autumn, I enrolled in the dental school of the University of Pennsylvania. (As part of the application process for the dental school, I had to carve a piece of chalk to show my manual dexterity — a test that I passed.)

Between my father and me, we paid up front for a year's tuition, plus room and board. It was no small investment. I remember carving my initials, L. C., into roughly twelve hundred dollars' worth of dental equipment. This was at a time when the average annual household income nationwide was just about $6,000. But it was seen as an investment in my future, and I gather my father rather liked the idea of "my son, the dentist."

You can imagine his response when, about eight days into my dental courses, I began to have doubts about whether dentistry was the right fit for me. I decided that I wanted to go back to Hunter to finish my fourth year unencumbered by any specific career decision and only then make up my mind about dental school or some other path forward. This was pure intuition on my part — just a gut feeling, but nevertheless quite real.

Of course, I got a lot of flack and pushback. My father was furious, in part because his dream of "my son, the dentist" seemed to be going out the window but also because all that money in tuition, tools, and room and board was going out the window with it. On top of my father's displeasure, the dean of the dental school was unnecessarily nasty to me. I wasn't sophisticated at the time, so I didn't have much to say back to him when he lectured me, trying to put me on a guilt trip, saying: "Mr. Cooperman, you have deprived the hundred-and-first applicant of a dental education." I wasn't savvy enough to realize that at only eight days into the semester, he could (and would) easily go to somebody on the waitlist and bring them in. Instead, I just stood there and took it.

The only one who supported my decision — besides, of course, Toby — was Hunter's dean of students, a wonderful man, Dr. Glen T. Nygreen. He understood how much criticism I'd drawn on myself. He congratulated me on what he called "a very courageous decision" and allowed me to matriculate back in.

Deciding to leave dental school was one of the best decisions I've ever made in my life, and it was all based on gut instinct. I've often said that whatever success I've enjoyed in life I can attribute to good luck, hard work, and intuition. And that's why I've always encouraged young people to trust their intuition.

When I returned to Hunter in the autumn of 1963, I was free to take just about any courses I cared to, since I'd already fulfilled all the requirements for my major. Once again, following my intuition, I enrolled in ten elective courses in economics, and I never looked back. In economics and finance, I found my niche, my passionate interest, and my natural talent. Whereas before I'd always had to work hard for grades, when it came to economics, it seemed like I had a natural gift, the same way others might have a gift for picking up languages, learning musical instruments, or painting. I found I was able to easily grasp complex concepts that often seem quite abstruse to other people, and I genuinely enjoyed the subject matter.

> I've often said that whatever success I've enjoyed in life I can attribute to good luck, hard work, and intuition.

By the end of the spring semester of 1964, when Toby and I were poised to graduate (and to get married), I was well established academically and an attractive candidate for the various employers who came to the campus on recruiting missions. Of course, despite my new interest in finance, I was still a kid with a chemistry major, and now that was my "strong suit" when seeking employment. That's why I eventually wound up at Xerox Corporation.

After I got through the first interview on the Hunter campus, they invited me up for a second interview at a manufacturing subsidiary in Webster, New York, just outside Rochester, where Xerox had its home office. The manager who interviewed me took me through some of the quality-control laboratories. At that time, their big machine was the Xerox 914. In the lab, they had about twenty of these machines sitting on platforms, running around the clock, printing out copies. He explained to me they were doing a study of the effect of the carbon-black particle size on toner consumption. The fused letters on the paper are comprised of carbon black. They could grind that to various diameters. They were trying to figure out what effect the particle size had on the number of copies per pound of toner used.

I said to him rather innocently, "I assume you find that the finer the particle size, the more copies you're getting per pound of toner."

He looked at me and said, "That's exactly what we're finding. Why did you say that?"

I answered, "Because the surface area of the molecule is greater."

I think it was perhaps because of this exchange, which appeared to have impressed the manager, that they gave me what I believe was the best offer they'd given anyone starting out from Hunter: roughly $7,000 per year to serve as a quality-control engineer. This was a good salary for a freshly minted graduate at that time.

So, as newlyweds, Toby and I got into my new 1964 Dodge Dart (retail base price $2,313) and headed upstate. At the same time, wanting to further my knowledge of finance, I enrolled in the University of Rochester Graduate School of Business, with my classes scheduled at night. I was ambitious and didn't mind the prospect of hard work on two fronts, the job and the master's program.

There was, however, a problem. A few weeks into my time at Xerox, my hours changed in a manner that had not been mentioned during my recruitment and that did not mesh well with my master's studies. The operation in which I was involved went to a twenty-four-hour work week. This meant that I was now expected to work a different eight hours every week. One week I'd work eight in the morning until four, the next week four in the afternoon until midnight, and the following week midnight until eight in the morning. The weeks that I had the four-to-midnight shift conflicted with my classes, so I had to find another young engineer with a similar situation and trade off with him: work sixteen hours, go to school; work sixteen hours, go to school. Toby, God bless her, finally said, "This is very hard. Why don't you go to school full-time and I'll work?" This opened the door to the next great chapter in my life — my studies at the Columbia Business School for my master's degree in business administration, which in turn set me on the path that has gotten me to where I am today.

CHAPTER 3

COLUMBIA BUSINESS SCHOOL

A teacher affects eternity: he can never tell where his influence stops.

— HENRY ADAMS

I was honored to serve on the Board of Overseers of the Columbia Business School for many years and, as of this writing, have only recently stepped down from that body. I have also been very pleased to be able to serve the school in other ways. In 2012, I made a $25 million gift to help underwrite the building of a new campus in Manhattanville. In 2007, I established the school's Cooperman Scholarship Challenge, creating more than forty need-based scholarships, and in 2000 I was happy to be able to create the Leon Cooperman Scholarship for students in need of further financial assistance, with an emphasis on graduates of New York City public schools. Earlier, in 1995, I endowed the Leon Cooperman Professorship in Finance and Economics.

Some people practice what they preach; I try to preach what I practice. "When you achieve financial security," I told a group of

Columbia MBA students in 2012, "give back to those who are less fortunate. When in a position to help others, do so…. [It is a] moral imperative to give others the opportunity to pursue the American dream."

> Some people practice what they preach; I try to preach what I practice.

During my time as a graduate student, Columbia provided me with an excellent business education, opened the door to my successful, nearly twenty-five-year career at Goldman Sachs, and was the place where I made friendships that have lasted my entire adult life. It has been both a pleasure and an honor to be able to give back and make sure other students following in my footsteps continue to have the opportunities that Columbia gave me.

The gifts I've described are ones I never could have imagined being capable of on that autumn day in 1965 when I first set foot on the Columbia campus. By then, Toby had taken a job as an employment counselor with the New York State Department of Unemployment. It was she who was going to support the household while I worked on my MBA degree — doing so on an expedited, trimester, sixteen-month schedule in order to graduate as soon as possible, at the end of January 1967.

We moved into a very modest one-bedroom apartment at 6141 Broadway in The Bronx, with a monthly rent of $110. Shortly after, once our first son was born, we'd bite the bullet, roll the dice, and step up to a two-bedroom apartment in the same building, for which we paid what then seemed like a whopping $130 a month.

As an aside, I've got a funny story about that apartment building that I'll share before talking about business school. As I say, the building was modest, nothing like what you'd find a few blocks away in ritzy Riverdale. But it was nice enough and clean. Anyway, our building superintendent was a big fan of ping-pong, so much so that he'd set up a ping-pong table in the basement of the building and welcomed all challengers. So sometimes, on an evening or a weekend, I'd go down there and play against him. One time while I was down there, the phone rang, and it was a deliveryman asking for the building's address. The superintendent gave him the address, but instead of saying "Bronx" he said "Riverdale." After that I thought, "Well, if the building super says he lives in Riverdale, then I'm going to say that I live in Riverdale." I felt as if I'd come up in the world, without even trying.

I made several very close friendships among my fellow MBA candidates, guys who remained my friends throughout the years that followed. Two were Mario Gabelli and Arthur Samberg. Both lived near Toby and me in the vicinity of Van Cortlandt Park. Mario, Art, and I often commuted to the campus together, either on the subway or, when the subway workers went on strike, by carpooling. Another was a young man from Sunnyside Queens who, like Mario and Art, would go on to leave big tracks in the world of finance — Spencer Davidson.

Mario came from a working-class Italian family in The Bronx. His Italian-immigrant Gabelli grandparents had somehow wound up in the coal country of western Pennsylvania, where his grandfather died in a coal-mining accident. After that, Mario's grandmother took her two-year-old son, Joseph, back to Italy, where he was raised before immigrating to The Bronx with his Italian wife. Joseph subsequently worked as a cook at Manhattan's famed Lüchow's Restaurant.

Mario attended Fordham Prep and then Fordham University on a scholarship, where he studied accounting and philosophy and earned a *summa cum laude* degree in business administration. As a kid, he had developed a fascination with stocks and investing. He'd been just twelve or so when he started hitchhiking up to Westchester to caddy at fancy, private country clubs. While caddying, he would listen to the Wall Streeters talk about investments and trading, and he fell in love with the business. He was investing in stocks while still in elementary school.

Mario, who has remained a lifelong friend, went on to become a multibillionaire investor and money manager, most notably through the well-known Gabelli Mutual Funds and GAMCO Investors. Like me, he has been an active philanthropist, giving many millions to Fordham University, Boston College, Roger Williams University, the University of Miami, and the University of Nevada (Reno), among other institutions and organizations, including, of course, Columbia Business School.

Arthur Samberg, who sadly died from cancer in July 2020, spent his first eight years in The Bronx, just four blocks from Yankee Stadium. After that, his family moved to New Jersey. His father was an electrician. He was quite tall — six feet, seven inches — so of course, he played basketball in high school. And he was smart — quite literally a rocket scientist.

Before he showed up at Columbia, Art had already taken a degree in aeronautics and astronautics at MIT and had worked for three years at Lockheed Martin's Palo Alto campus as a satellite-control systems engineer. There, he helped develop the Polaris missile while also earning an MS from Stanford. After that, however, the engineering community's loss became the financial community's gain, when Art developed a fascination with the stock market and got himself to Columbia, never looking back. Like Mario and me, Arthur eventually became a billionaire through the firm he founded, Pequot Capital Management — always, at the same time, keeping up with his basketball, with a full court installed next door to the trading floor at Pequot.

He never stopped, whether at work or at leisure. He climbed Mount Kilimanjaro in 2000 to celebrate his fifty-ninth birthday. And he gave back: $25 million to Columbia Business School, another $25 million to the New York-Presbyterian Morgan Stanley Children's Hospital, and many millions more to dozens of other charities.

Spencer Davidson came from Sunnyside, Queens. He'd attended Stuyvesant High School, which remains today one of the finest high schools in the New York City school system. He then graduated from Queens College, which he attended at night while maintaining a full-time job, with a degree in economics. He also held a job when I first met him at Columbia, managing a ladies' clothing store near the campus.

Spencer went on to successful stints at Brown Brothers Harriman, Beck Mack & Oliver, and Odyssey Investment Partners before joining the General American Investors Company, where he has risen to the post of chairman of the board. Like the rest of us, Spencer has been deeply involved in charitable giving, donating both his money and his talents to such organizations as San Diego's Neurosciences Research Foundation.

To say that we received first-class educations in the graduate business program at Columbia would be an understatement. All our professors were excellent, and at least one was nothing short of a living legend of finance.

Roger Murray taught securities analysis. In addition to being our senior by many years (old enough to be my father), Murray was also different from Gabelli, Samberg, Davidson, and me in that he came from a wealthy background and was therefore something of a blue blood. He'd been educated at the elite Phillips Academy and then

Yale, graduating Phi Beta Kappa in 1932 before earning an MBA and then a PhD from the New York University Graduate School of Business Administration. Before coming to Columbia, he'd been a vice president at Bankers Trust, where he'd made a specialty of investment strategy.

At Columbia, where he arrived in 1956, he served as associate dean, S. Sloan Colt professor of banking and finance, and eventually professor emeritus and distinguished lecturer before retiring in 1978. In addition to his teaching, Murray was at various times an key advisor to government officials and politicians on important financial matters. For example, he invented the idea of the individual retirement account (IRA) in 1962 and was a strong advocate for the Keogh Act, which enabled tax-deferred pension accounts for self-employed individuals.

In his teaching, Murray was a firm devotee of the value-investing philosophy espoused by Benjamin Graham and David Dodd in their seminal 1934 text *Security Analysis*.[2] In fact, Murray was so much an evangelist for Graham and Dodd's thinking that it was he who (along with Charles Sidney Cottle and Frank Block) eventually got called upon to revise and update later editions of their book. Graham and Dodd had both in their time taught at Columbia. Warren Buffett had been one of Graham's star students some sixteen years before I arrived on campus.

Graham and Dodd's methodology of value investing involves scrutinizing the business fundamentals underlying any given stock, and in that manner identifying those securities that are intrinsically undervalued. This rigorous process results in minimizing the specu-

---

2   In *The Intelligent Investor* (1949), Graham took the high-level academic ideas described in *Security Analysis* and made them accessible for a popular audience. Through multiple editions and translations, the book has sold more than a million copies worldwide and remains in print to this day, as does *Security Analysis*.

lative aspect of purchasing a security, replacing it with a reasoned, evidence-based prospect of a positive financial result.

In imparting the tactics and tools of value-related security analysis, Murray was punctilious about details and always quite demanding of his students. He was, I would say, the ultimate practitioner. I remember submitting a paper to him in which I did a comparative analysis of two textile firms, Burlington Industries and J.P. Stevens. As part of my analysis, I presented twenty different ratios showing results over a ten-year period. This represented something like two or three hundred calculations in total. In all that maze of numbers, I made one mistake (a transposition error), and Murray caught it. That's how good he was, and that's how much of a stickler he was when it came to details. Murray gave only two A grades in that class. I got one of them; the other went to Mario.

Another truly outstanding professor was Reynold Sachs. He was actually just a few years older than Mario, Art, Spencer, and me, having received a BA in economics from Oberlin in 1961, an MA in economics from Northwestern in 1962, and a PhD in economics from Columbia in 1965. Sachs taught us two courses that were required for MBA students: Business Economics, which was Columbia's fancy term for macroeconomics, and Managerial Economics, which was Columbia-speak for microeconomics.

Sachs was a superb teacher, and we all came away from his class a lot more knowledgeable than when we went into it (which was, of course, the idea). Sachs left Columbia not long after we graduated, did a stint in the Pentagon as deputy assistant secretary of defense from 1967 through 1969, and eventually got a JD from Georgetown. He later made a fortune with his firm Digital Switch Corporation, which was acquired by the French firm Alcatel in a $4.4 billion stock swap deal in 1998.

In 2017, at the fiftieth reunion of our MBA class of 1967, Mario, Art, and I, along with Spencer Davidson, sat on a panel where we discussed Columbia Business School and its impact on each of us. At one point, the moderator commented that there must have been "something in the water" at Columbia that year in that it produced four of the most successful investors of the era. With that I raised my hand and stopped the discussion. "There wasn't something in the water," I said. "The 'something' was our faculty, the most important of whom was Professor Reynold Sachs, who is sitting right down here in the front row." With that, Sachs got a loud, well-deserved round of applause from the assembly.

Finally, I absolutely must mention another influential teacher: Jack Zwick, professor of finance and international business who later was a professor of business at the George Washington University and the founding director of the World Trade Institute. In fact, it would be Jack Zwick who, fortuitously, would help open the door to what became my very successful, twenty-five-year career with Goldman Sachs, the next great chapter in my business life.

This brings me to another point. Neither Mario, Spencer, nor I possessed undergraduate degrees from any Ivy League schools. And even Art's degree from MIT wasn't in economics or business, but rather aeronautics. Without having gotten our "tickets punched," as the saying goes, at Columbia, we never would have gotten entrée to the upper echelons of the financial world.

I explained this to a young lady in 2015, during a Q&A session when I, among others, was inducted at the Sixty-eighth Annual Horatio Alger Awards in Washington, DC. An undergraduate, she asked me what I thought was the value of a degree from a lesser-known university as opposed to a degree from a "name" university. I replied, "I have to be very careful how I answer this. You know,

I basically consider myself a street kid, and I owe a great debt to Hunter College. I got a fabulous education there. But I don't think, unfortunately, I could have gotten into Wall Street and pursued the career that I pursued with just a degree from the City University of New York. I know I never would have gotten in the door at Goldman Sachs without my MBA from Columbia. I'm not a snob, but the fact is that a degree from a major university is indeed more valuable than a degree from someplace else, at least when you are talking about Wall Street. It's unfortunate that I have to say that, but it is generally true. I myself hire *people*, not résumés. My model for hiring is 'outside the box' as regards the general practice at big firms. And I prefer PhDs, which I define as people who are *poor, hungry*, and *driven*. But the fact is I personally never would have been able to make my important next step without that degree from Columbia."

I opened this chapter with a quote from Henry Adams: "A teacher affects eternity: he can never tell where his influence stops." Certainly, the influence of our professors at Columbia has never stopped. I would like to say that they endowed us with the intelligence and work ethic that have been the foundations of our success, but frankly we all had both already or we never would have gotten to Columbia in the first place. What our Columbia professors really endowed us with were the critical skills necessary to succeed in the financial markets and, of course, those "golden tickets" to Wall Street, otherwise known as Columbia MBAs.

PART II

GOLDMAN YEARS

CHAPTER 4

EARLY YEARS AT GOLDMAN SACHS

What you get by achieving your goals is not as important
as what you become by achieving your goals.

— HENRY DAVID THOREAU

When I graduated from the Columbia Business School, I was one of the top students in my class and a member of Beta Gamma Sigma, the International Business Honor Society. To be admitted to this society, you must be in the top 20 percent of your class. When recruiters came from the Wall Street firms to interview and scout new employees, I was an attractive package. GPA aside, I'd earned straight As in finance and had won the *Wall Street Journal* Student Achievement Award.

I wound up with sixteen job offers, including one from Goldman Sachs, which, although attractive at $12,500, was not my best offer from a starting-salary perspective. This was no small matter to me at the time, as I was broke, in debt (with a hefty student loan), and had the responsibilities of a wife and newborn son.

I'd liked everyone I'd met at Goldman during the interview process. I also liked what I sensed about the atmosphere of the organization. One of my professors, Jack Zwick, was friendly with Goldman's vice president in charge of administration, Robert McElfresh. It was through Zwick that I got the interview with McElfresh, which was followed by an interview with the head of research at Goldman, Bob Danforth. It was Danforth who made me the offer to join the firm. But because of the salary issue, I hesitated, and for the first and only time in my life, I missed a deadline to respond. So Danforth called me and said, "We're disappointed we haven't heard from you."

I explained my dilemma: I thought Goldman was a great firm, and I thought I could succeed and be happy there, but I had no money in the bank, a wife and child to support, and a large loan to repay. I was also blunt about the fact that I had more lucrative offers in hand. I asked Danforth, "Do you think I can be making $25,000 a year in five years?" (I used that number because, assuming a 15 percent raise year-over-year for five years, you get to just over $25,000 from a starting point of $12,500.)

Danforth replied, "If you work hard and keep your nose clean, I think you can do it." My intuition told me to go ahead and accept the offer. As it turned out, I wound up making $180,000 in my fifth year.

I graduated from Columbia with my MBA on January 31, 1967, and started working at Goldman as a junior analyst the very next day. Danforth turned out to be a great boss and a great mentor. He hailed from Yankton, South Dakota, where he was born in 1926. After getting an economics degree from Oberlin in 1947 and an MBA from the University of Michigan in 1948, he'd joined Goldman in 1948 and became a partner in 1963. He was to remain the partner-in-charge of investment research until 1976. He thereafter continued as a limited partner and an important consultant and advisor to the firm. Sadly, he passed away in 1987.

Another future Goldman star who joined the firm about the same time I did was Roy Smith. Roy was a graduate of the United States Naval Academy, and he came to Goldman with a newly minted MBA from Harvard. Roy was destined to enjoy a twenty-year career with the firm, eventually becoming senior international partner and president of Goldman Sachs International, based out of London. When he departed the firm in 1987, Roy went on to join the faculty of the NYU Stern School of Business, where he became professor of entrepreneurship and finance, occupying a chair endowed by my good friend Ken Langone, a noted philanthropist and cofounder of Home Depot. Roy remained at Stern until retiring in 2017. He died two years later.

In joining Goldman, I was stepping into a distinguished, if arduous, corporate tradition. Founded in 1869, Goldman remains, even to this day, one of the most powerful, profitable, and respected financial institutions on the planet. In fact, of all the firms that made me offers out of school, it is today the only one never to have been merged or absorbed out of existence, successfully bucking what has emerged as a trend on Wall Street. As an example, look at the once-mighty Merrill Lynch, which is now a division of Bank of America.

I've used the word "arduous." Starting off as a junior analyst, the daily grind represented nothing less than indentured servitude. Twelve-hour days were not the exception but the rule, and sixteen-hour days were not uncommon. Individuals were expected to go the extra mile and excel while at the same time always being a part of the team. The idea was that only by moving the firm and your colleagues forward could you move yourself forward. As Roy Smith once said regarding the firm, "We tended to resent heroes if any were to emerge because we all knew that it was the team approach, the phalanx, that made the difference ... plus not letting our egos get out of line. We produced a somewhat hard-to-classify mystique of efficiency without too much identity. That sometimes frustrated us when we felt we had a lesser public image than some of us from time to time would like to have seen."

As I told Charles Ellis back in 2007, when he was researching his book about Goldman, *The Partnership*, balance and cooperation were key. More than any other firm on Wall Street, Goldman had terrific organizational and strategic balance across all sectors. It was a finely-tuned, well-oiled, and highly collaborative and cooperative environment. Every employee pulled on their own individual oar, but all pulled together toward common goals. Everybody belonged to, and believed in, "the team." Of course, there was some politics — isn't there always? — but not nearly as much as in most other firms.

Nothing short of individual excellence was expected, and demanded. The firm's management didn't give out any trophies for doing a good job — that was a given, or you wouldn't be around for long — but there *was* much unwelcome attention to endure regarding any failings you might have, any business you might blow, or anything about your style or productivity that wasn't of the caliber expected. So, along with team spirit, there was fear and accountability. You would never dare leave something undone that you should have attended to. You were responsible for being the best at handling and serving each client and for doing the most with your accounts. A very Darwinian environment.

Of course, team or no team, the competition to eventually achieve a partnership position was quite intense. But it was only by demonstrating your ability to be productive within the team, working collaboratively with others, that you could make yourself stand out and hope for a partnership slot, the ultimate "golden ticket."

Two years after I joined the firm, New Orleans native Gus Levy became senior partner and chairman, replacing Sidney Weinberg who retired that year after beginning his career at Goldman as a $3-per-week assistant janitor in 1907. Levy, at the start of his Goldman career in 1933, had perhaps seemed as unlikely a superstar as Weinberg. A college dropout, he'd joined the firm at twenty-three to head a one-man trading department, for which he was paid the grand sum of $27.50 a week. He ran and greatly expanded the trading department through 1969, when he ascended to the chairmanship. During that time, he worked closely with his young protégé Bob Mnuchin, among others, to develop a range of new and sophisticated trading practices, among them block trading — high-volume transactions in a specific security traded on behalf of institutional clients, privately executed outside of the open market for the security in question.

Levy was innovative in other ways, too, as when he founded Goldman's eight-man "management committee" formed of seven highly experienced, senior banking partners who acted as a *de facto* corporate board, with Gus presiding as the eighth and predominant member. Levy was also, by turns, tough, taciturn, generous, short-tempered, gregarious, critical, and encouraging. In short, his various and sometimes contradictory moods matched the "vibe" at Goldman perfectly: *perform*.

Unlike his trading mentor, Levy, my friend Bob Mnuchin was a Yale graduate (1955). Thus, like me and other hires of the 1950s and 1960s, he came to the firm with excellent academic credentials. This has sometimes seemed to me somewhat ironic given the modest educational backgrounds of Weinberg and Levy. One could still, of course, start at the firm with a minimum of education and begin by mopping floors, as Weinberg had. But by the time Mnuchin and I, and our generation, came on to the scene, the most a newly hired janitor could hope for would be to one day become senior janitor; the sky was no longer the limit.

Mnuchin was named a general partner the year I arrived at Goldman. By 1976, the year I would make partner, he'd be running the Trading and Arbitrage Division and would eventually join the management committee in 1980, remaining there until his retirement ten years later. He and I have remained good friends through the years, and I'm delighted to see him still going strong at age eighty-nine.

During my tenure, I often worked closely with Roy Zuckerberg, who'd joined Goldman the same year I did and who, at the prompting of Robert Menschel, did a terrific job expanding Goldman's servicing of wealthy individual investors through the newly-formed Private Client Services Division. At Roy's behest, I attended many carefully orchestrated dinners that he organized with groups of potential clients. My mission was to impress them with the depth and clarity of research analysis they could expect from Goldman as it influenced portfolio strategy. I gather that Roy also liked that I could easily "switch-hit," moving off statistics-heavy jargon and into well-timed and well-aimed light banter and jokes whenever necessary. This was generally a large social aspect to obtaining and maintaining new clients, whether individual or institutional. That's still very much the case today. Personal relationships bolster business relationships.

I and my research colleague, Gary Wenglowski, among others, were often "on the road," reaching out to institutional clients to discuss research, macroeconomics, and portfolio logistics. In fact, we spent a great deal of time on the institutional investor circuit, bouncing between New York, Boston, Hartford, Philadelphia, Minneapolis,

Chicago, San Francisco, Los Angeles, Denver, Houston, Dallas, and Atlanta. We also traveled to Europe twice a year, where we made stops in all the major financial centers: London, Paris, Zurich, etc. Local Goldman reps in each city would set up a string of appointments with institutional clients (or potential clients), running from breakfast through dinner. Then the next day, it would be on to the next city.

Selling the soundness, thoroughness, and integrity of Goldman's research was a key part of selling the rest of the firm's other products and services. Largely for this reason, Goldman's "house accounting" was set up so that the Banking Division paid 50 percent of the total cost of running the Research Division. It was realized that the banking managers were all generalists who absolutely needed the support of research to give them a competitive edge when making calls on clients and prospects.

The job of a research analyst, and the mission of a research division, is quite complex, involving a broad set of skills. Specializing in specific industries, analysts must not only become experts on market conditions and corporate details in their niche; they must also initiate, build, and maintain close relationships with their counterpart institutional analysts and portfolio managers, as well as key industry contacts in the fields they cover, and collaborate with sales and account people who utilize and merchandize their analyses.

I did well. For nine years running, I was voted the number-one portfolio strategist in the *Institutional Investor* All-America Research Team survey. I built my reputation both within and outside Goldman. This was desired by the firm. In fact, it was a guiding principle of the business that every analyst should try to build their own personal brand, their own personal reputation, in their own research niches and categories. The (successful) ambition of the firm was to be seen as home to an elite team of superstar analysts and strategists — the best in the business, a true "brain trust," if you will. This indeed became a large part of the face of the organization, one that attracted and retained both institutional and individual clients. In 1972, I was made head of research under Danforth as partner-in-charge of the division.

Four years later, following the death of Gus Levy, John L. Weinberg and John C. Whitehead (who became known in the firm as "the two Johns"), were named coheads (co–senior partners) of Goldman. They both had long tenures with the firm. The son of Sidney Weinberg, John Weinberg had been born in 1925 and joined the firm after serving in World War II and graduating with a master's degree from Harvard Business School. Whitehead, born in 1922 and another veteran, followed him in 1950 after earning the same degree from the same institution. They both rose rapidly through Goldman's Investment Banking Division and were made partners in 1956. As coheads of Goldman, the two Johns were to lead the firm into its greatest and most profitable period up to that date. At the end of 1976, Goldman was coming off the best year in its history, earing approximately $40 million pretax, and the future was full of promise. Growth was the order of the day.

Thanksgiving 1976 swung around and, as had become my habit on that holiday, I took the Friday off to be with my family, even though the markets and my office were open. I was relaxing when I answered the phone and found the two Johns on the line. They'd chosen that day to notify staff as to which lucky few would be made partners that year. It seemed I had made the list. I was to receive three-quarters of a percentage point of profits in my first year as partner — to be reinvested, as was the custom, in the firm. (By 1991, when Goldman's pretax profits were $1.8 billion, I'd be participating at the rate of 1.75 percent.) But as John Whitehead reminded me on that phone call, "Now, you'll *really* have to start to work."

And he wasn't kidding.

CHAPTER 5

PARTNERSHIP YEARS AT GOLDMAN SACHS

Your work is going to fill a large part of your life, and the only way to be truly satisfied is to do what you believe is great work. And the only way to do great work is to love what you do.

— STEVE JOBS

In many high-end law firms, "making partner" signals an end to the heaviest lifting, a time to get out from under the grunt work and leave that to more junior members of staff. Not so in most investment institutions, and certainly not so at the Goldman Sachs of my era. In the culture of Goldman, being made partner meant ramping up from what in practical terms had probably been a sixty-hour week to something closer to an eighty-hour week. (It was no accident that the two Johns had telephoned me on the Friday after Thanksgiving to invite me to become a partner while I was taking a four-day weekend to be with my family. They were working.)

Goldman had never tolerated any member of staff who displayed a mere nine-to-five/work-for-hire mindset. Anyone like that could anticipate a very short career there. Goldman instead expected utter devotion to the firm, as well as to personal, professional, and corporate excellence. And they expected it from everyone.

> To those scheduled to get the largest percentage of the spoils also went the ultimate responsibility to do everything possible to maximize the firm's profitability.

With partners, the firm doubled down on these expectations. To those scheduled to get the largest percentage of the spoils also went the ultimate responsibility to do everything possible to maximize the firm's profitability. Bedside phones rang at every hour of the night as market events around the globe rose up to demand attention. Planes, trains, and hotels became second homes. Vacations became pipe dreams (although visions of vast wealth at the end of a Goldman partnership career certainly did not).

But I'm not complaining. I and my fellow workaholics certainly enjoyed the ride.

* * *

While running Goldman's research, and even after I'd given up that role, one of my favorite companies and favorite stocks through the 1960s, '70s, and '80s was the technology-oriented conglomerate Teledyne, headed by its brilliant, reclusive, and often contrarian cofounder, Dr. Henry E. Singleton, a talented electrical engineer but more importantly an elusive legend in management and Wall Street circles. Throughout his long career, Singleton consciously decentralized his organization (thus flying in the face of a management truth that many of his CEO peers thought to be gospel), shunned rather than courted Wall Street analysts, never paid a dividend until early 1987, ignored many opportunities to justify a stock split, and made a religion of repurchasing his shares whenever a good opportunity arose. At the same time, over three decades, he grew the value of the firm at an unprecedented rate, weathering every market boom and bust — a run that would end only with the cruel bear winter of the early 1990s.

This is a feat that Dr. Singleton accomplished largely by fixating on capital allocation. As Warren Buffett commented in 1980, "Henry Singleton has the best operating and capital deployment record in American business.... If one took the 100 top business school graduates and made a composite of their triumphs, their record would not be as good as Singleton's."

Singleton is the single greatest industrialist I've ever met (and I've met plenty). He knew how to move between real assets and financial assets in a way you don't see today. In his time, he masterminded scores of major acquisitions and made Teledyne a major investor in numerous other concerns. All the while, he oversaw Teledyne's core business of technological development, including designing an inertial guidance system still used in military and commercial aircraft.

Dr. Singleton and Teledyne represent one of the most profound managerial and entrepreneurial success stories in the annals of modern business history. Simply stated, Singleton always followed the principal of allocating cash to assets in a way that offered, in his view, the highest potential return given the investment risk involved. Singleton did not, like other CEOs, restrict himself only to real assets but rather took advantage of returns in financial markets *along with* the real sector. In this, he was both a visionary and a virtuoso.

Dr. Singleton had left Litton Industries in 1958 after being passed over for president and, along with Litton colleague George Kozmetzky who had also left the firm, launched Teledyne. *Teledyne* is the contraction of two Greek words, "tele" (distance) and "dyne" (force). So, the literal translation is "force at a distance". The name is more than apropos.

I was first attracted to Teledyne when I observed the high returns on capital that the company generated in competitive businesses, leading to a large free cash flow which the subsidiaries returned to the home office, cash that Singleton was free to apply as he saw fit. Between roughly 1960 and 1968, Teledyne did about 130 acquisitions, following a traditional roll-up model. In 1968, Singleton determined that it made little sense to use undervalued public equity to pay private market prices to acquire companies — a disciplined and correct call. In other words, Singleton recognized the unusually low cost of equity capital the company enjoyed and used Teledyne's common stock as a currency to complete acquisitions. His theory paid off. During this period of acquisition, the firm's net income increased from almost nothing to more than $58 million in 1969.

From 1972 through 1984, Singleton did eight self-tender offers, retiring about 90 percent of the company's stock but never selling a share of his own. By reducing share count, he went from being a one percent owner to being a 20 percent owner. On three occasions, he offered bonds in return for stock, always correctly playing the interest rate cycle.

In the years 1971 through 1981, Teledyne's return on equity ranged from 25 percent to 30 percent, both approaching twice that of American industry as a whole. During the same period, each line of Teledyne's manufacturing sector earned more than 50 percent before taxes on identifiable assets, with pretax profit margins in the manufacturing sector averaging about 15 percent. Additionally, because of his extremely well-timed stock repurchases, Singleton in the same years dramatically increased earnings per share. In fact, his earnings-per-share growth came in at about twice that of net income growth.

A good example of Dr. Singleton's contrarian smarts is that when many other firms (particularly insurance companies) invested in long-term bonds in the wake of the brutal 1973/1974 bear market, Teledyne, which held two insurance firms in its portfolio, went the other way. Singleton saw stocks as being fundamentally more attractive than bonds, given the current market realities, and that stocks contained a far greater potential for both capital appreciation and growth of income going forward. He bought large, concentrated positions in assorted companies, including Litton Industries, Curtiss-Wright, Brockway Glass, and Reichhold Chemical. He simply recognized that bonds were riskier than stocks — another brilliant insight, in retrospect.

An additional pillar of Dr. Singleton's success was that he routinely built cash with which to deal with any eventuality in the marketplace. In early 1982, American industry as a whole languished in the most illiquid financial position and highest debt load since 1945. Conversely, Teledyne was cash rich — a direct result of Singleton's correct assessment of market realities, and market direction, one year earlier. At the start of May 1982, Teledyne had on-hand cash and equivalents of nearly $1 billion, possessed zero bank debt, and was looking at less than $5 million per year in maturing long-term debt scheduled for the next decade. At the same time, the conglomerate was also generating approximately $400 million in annual cash flow.

Given all this, I became more than annoyed when the May 31, 1982, issue of *Business Week* carried a highly critical profile of Teledyne and Dr. Singleton, making arguments to which I took strong exception. The writer of the piece grossly misrepresented Singleton's business strategies and practices, simplistically (and misleadingly) attributing the firm's success to no more than a voracious acquisition habit in the 1960s and a manic stock-buying habit in the 1970s – an absurd, reductionist portrayal of Singleton's overall program of management and investment. Even the cover illustration was an insult: a depiction of Singleton as the mythical Greek character Icarus, who flew too close to the sun on wax wings and fell to the earth when they melted. Singleton's wings were made of far more resilient stuff.

I wasted no time in expressing my concerns and criticisms in a seven-page open letter to the editor of *Business Week*, which I also shared with numerous Goldman Sachs clients:

> I have been a reader of your publication for about 20 years, and only on one previous occasion (cover story, "Death of Equities," August 13, 1979) was I sufficiently aroused to write to the Editor. Now your May 31, 1982 cover story on Teledyne, Inc. and its chairman, Dr. Henry Singleton, is a second such occasion.
>
> I found the article to demonstrate a blatant lack of understanding of this company (bordering on the irresponsible in its thrust) as well as a lack of appreciation of what, in my opinion, is one of the greatest managerial success stories in the annals of modern business history. The reporter simply portrays the company's success to date as the result of an acquisition binge in the 1960s and a stock-buying surge in the 1970s, the latter being financed by "siphoning" off the cash flow of its operating businesses to get where it is today. These are gross simplifications of rather elaborate, well-conceived, and, most importantly,

well-executed business judgments and strategies for better than 20 years.

Speaking in general terms, Dr. Singleton has followed the principle of allocating cash to assets (real or financial) that offer, in his view, the highest potential return given the investment risk involved. You criticize this shifting of capital from real to financial assets. An intelligent investor would recognize that, in point of fact, that is precisely the responsibility of management. More importantly, Dr. Singleton has not, as have many other chief executive officers, restricted himself solely to real assets but rather has built a company able to take advantage of returns in both financial markets and the real sector.

More specifically, as a Teledyne observer, I can identify at least five different strategies utilized to foster the company's development over the past 20 years.

Strategy One: Growth Through Acquisition

In the period 1960–1969, Dr. Singleton recognized the unusually low cost of equity capital the company enjoyed and relentlessly used the company's common stock as a currency to acquire. In this period of acquisition growth (in excess of 130 acquisitions), the company's sales and net income increased from essentially zero to about $1.3 billion and $58.1 million, respectively.

Strategy Two: Intensively Manage Your Business

In the period of 1970–1981, Dr. Singleton *and his management team* demonstrated an ability to manage second to none. *Net income, without* the benefit of *any* acquisitions, rose from $61.9 million in 1970 (a peak year) to $4,412.3 million in 1981, a compound growth of approximately 19%. (In that period, the S&P 400 earnings grew at a 12% rate off a depressed base.) Net income of the 100% owned manufacturing businesses rose more than sixfold in that period, to $269.6 million from $46.7 million. The company's ratios of profitability are among the best in American industry — return on equity ranged for 25% to 30%. In the past few years, and its return on total capital exceeds 20%, both approaching twice that of American industry. In the last few years, each line of business in the company's manufacturing sector has earned in *excess* of 50% before taxes on identifiable assets, with pretax profit margins in the manufacturing sector in the area of 15%.

Do you possibly believe that this record of growth and profitability could be achieved in a competitive world economy with a tactic of "siphoning-off" the operating earnings to finance the build-up of a stock portfolio? Doubtful. And in fact, the company while not one of the more aggressive spenders on plant and equipment, has spent well in excess of its cumulative depreciation in the period of 1973–1981. More to the point, I would suggest that a conservative approach to capital additions may have been more appropriate given the economic realities of the world economy, which is today awash with excess capacity and it likely to recover in a sluggish fashion.

Strategy Three: Repurchase Your Undervalued Equity

Just as Dr. Singleton recognized he had an unusually attractive stock to trade with in the 1960s, he developed the belief that the company's shares were undervalued in the 1970s. In the period 1971–1980, you correctly point out that the company repurchased approximately 75% of its shares. What you did not point out is that despite the stock's 32% drop from its all-time high reached in mid-1981 to the time of your article, the stock price remains well above the highest price paid by the company (and multiples above the average price paid) in this ten-year period. Contrary to many corporate managements whose stock repurchases have proven ill-timed, Teledyne has been extremely astute from both a stock market standpoint and a return on investment approach. The effect on earnings per share has been dramatic, with earnings-per-share growth about twice that of net income in the 1971–1981 period.

Strategy Four: Stocks Preferable to Bonds for the Taxable Investor

You seem to miss the key aspect of Dr. Singleton's emphasis of common stocks in early 1976. In owning an insurance company, Teledyne, like other insurance companies, has to invest its cash flow and can do so in a number of different financial and non-financial assets.

At a time when most insurance companies were still reeling from the devastating effects of the vicious 1973/74 bear market and were busy buying 9.5%–10% long-term bonds over common stocks, Teledyne determined that stocks were more attractive than bonds — particularly on an after tax basis given the tax preferred nature of dividend income from one corporation to another (85% excluded) and the better prospect of capital appreciation and income growth over time. The record thus far suggests that management's judgment was correct. The spread in asset performance is dramatic and quite relevant given the size of the company's asset base.

Lastly, I would point out the current market value of Teledyne's invested assets in stocks and fixed maturity investments is substantially above its cost basis — a situation very few insurance companies enjoy today because few had his prescience to emphasize stocks over bonds.

Strategy Five: Build Cash for Uncertain Times

At a time when American industry is saddled with the most illiquid financial position and highest debt load in the post–World War II period, Teledyne is in its most liquid financial position ever. I can assure you it is not an accident but rather the result of a correct assessment some 12 months ago of our current economic problems. The company currently has cash and equivalents of nearly $1 billion, no bank debt, and less than $5 million *per year* of maturing long-term debt in the ten-year period, 1984–1993. In addition, at recent levels of profitability, the company (excluding non-cash equity accounting earnings) generates approximately $400 million per year of cash flow.

In sum, then, you can see the company has utilized not only a multiplicity of strategies (as opposed to just two), but the timing of their adoption has been nothing short of brilliant. While I (and they) will readily concede to having their share of mistakes (International Harvester being the most visible), your article chose to concentrate on what appears to be a half-dozen examples of isolated difficulties without any consideration to the overwhelming successes of the company. Their record of *operating* and *asset management* is second to none. Their strategy in no way has been completely "hooked to cash" as you portray, and I believe your article is a poor excuse for good journalism and borders on a betrayal of the public confidence. While a more effusive person could have "pumped up" your writer, Dr. Singleton marches to his own drummer with a concentration of blood around his brain not his mouth.

The cover picture of the May 31st edition portrays Dr. Singleton as the mythical Greek character, Icarus, who fell to his death when he flew too close to the sun and his wax wing melted. However, I see Dr. Singleton (and his management team) as a group of exceedingly competent industrialists, working for the benefit of the Teledyne shareholder (yes, I am one of them), and my only regret is that I cannot find more Henry Singletons and Teledynes in which to invest.

After reading my analysis, Warren Buffett wrote me a note, which to this day I have framed upon a wall in my office:

Dear Lee,

I always enjoy both the quality of your writing and the quality of your thinking. Your letter to *Business Week* regarding Teledyne was 100% on the mark.

Best regards,
Warren

During the autumn of 2007, I gave a speech to the Value Investing Congress in which I specifically referenced and praised Dr. Singleton when criticizing the current manner in which stock buybacks were being deployed. Writing me after the speech, Warren concurred once again in my assessment of Singleton and of contemporary buybacks:

Henry was a manager that all investors, CEOs, would be CEOs, and MBA students should study. In the end he was 100% rational and there are very few CEOs about whom I can make that statement.

The stock repurchase situation is fascinating to me. That's because the answer is so simple. You do it when you are buying dollar bills at a clear cut and significant discount and *only* then.

As a general observation I would say that most companies that repurchased shares thirty years ago were doing it for the right reasons and most companies doing it now are wrong when doing so. Time after time I see managers who are attempting to be "fashionable" or, perhaps subconsciously, hoping to support their stock. Loews is a great example of a company that has always repurchased shares for the right reason. I could give examples of the reverse, but I try to follow the dictum "praise by name, criticize by category."

Best regards,
Warren

That dictum, by the way, is one that I follow as well: praise by name, criticize by category. Except, perhaps, when you feel an obligation to defend the reputation of one of the most truly brilliant entrepreneurs, managers, industrialists, and investors of the twentieth century. Also, as you'll see in future chapters, I don't feel the rule applies when I have a bone to pick with particular federal prosecutors, regulators, and members of Congress who have shown no reluctance in criticizing me by name. But all that is for later.

About two years before Dr. Singleton's death, in 1999, from a malignant brain tumor (and after a 1996 merger of Teledyne with Allegheny Ludlum), Singleton, who had remained on the Board but stepped down as chairman in 1991, participated in plans to break the conglomerate. He explained to me that he thought it was too difficult to find a manager who had the competency to manage so many diverse businesses under one roof, and that Teledyne never had a stock option plan because it made no sense to him to compensate the insurance executive for what the manufacturing executive created, and vice versa. Now that there would be focused entities, he would have stock option programs. Another benefit was that once the spin-off entities passed safe harbor, there would not be double taxation of the sold businesses.

* * *

In 1901, Andrew Carnegie funded the construction of a new engineering laboratory at the Stevens Institute of Technology in Hoboken, New Jersey, an institution he served as trustee. During his speech at the dedication of the lab, Carnegie stated that he hoped his tombstone might be inscribed with the words "Here lies a man who knew how to enlist in his service better men than himself." Every wise business leader should embrace this philosophy. I certainly do. And in this regard, I certainly hit the jackpot when I tapped the talents of Steven Einhorn, a truly great man of terrific smarts, quality, integrity, dedication, and judgment.

Steve and I first teamed up in 1977, when I, as the head of equity research at Goldman, hired him as a US equity portfolio strategist. He proved to be an invaluable lieutenant. Steve became a partner in 1986 and left as a limited partner at the end of 1998. Before that, he had advanced to become Goldman Sachs's partner-in-charge of the Global Investment Research Department and cochairman of the Investment Policy Committee. Prior to my hiring Steve at Goldman, he'd been manager of the Common Stock Department at the insurance company Prudential Financial. Before that, he'd received an MS in finance from the University of Illinois and a BA from Rutgers. All in all, I couldn't have picked a better man to be one of my key professional colleagues (and friends) going forward, not just at Goldman but also at my hedge fund, Omega Advisors, which I founded in 1991. Steve joined me there in 1999 as vice chairman after his retirement from Goldman.

Throughout his career at Goldman, Steve was widely followed by portfolio managers at banks, insurance companies, mutual funds, and a range of other investment organizations. And with good reason. For example, shortly before the blistering market crash of September 1987, which hardly anyone else saw coming, he told his clients to cut back their stock positions sharply.

I'll have more to say about Steve, and his pivotal role at Omega, in the next chapter. Suffice to say, for now, that he played a key role in my success during my later years at Goldman and subsequently at Omega. These days, now largely retired, Steve, like me and so many of our colleagues through the years, makes a habit of "giving back." Currently he is a member of the Board of Trustees of the Icahn School of Medicine at Mount Sinai and of Mount Sinai Hospital and also serves on their Investment Committee. As well, Steve is a member of the Investment Committee for the UJA-New York Federation, and with his wife, Shelly, engages in extensive direct philanthropy through the Einhorn Family Foundation, which they established in 1989.

* * *

In 1986, ten years after I'd been made partner, the incoming class of Goldman partners was the largest ever — thirty-seven, twice the size of any previous class — including two former Salomon Brothers managing directors (in other words, formal rivals of Goldman) and a prominent MIT professor, as well as, for the first time in Goldman history, a woman and a Black person. By now, Goldman's business was bigger than ever, a $38 billion concern. With size, the tight-knit culture of the firm had begun to change. As Lisa Endlich has written:

For the first time, existing partners had been unfamiliar with some of the candidates. The firm had grown and specialized. Its four divisions — equities (stock trading), investment banking, fixed income (bond trading), and J. Aron (currency and commodities trading) — had been separated into dozens of specialized departments, many members of which had very little contact with employees from outside their own department.... Impersonality had crept into the process. Perhaps the most atypical feature of the class of 1986 was the number of partners elevated from the ranks of salesmen and traders. Goldman Sachs's traditional strengths lay in the field of investment banking, in raising capital for large corporations or arranging mergers and acquisitions. Despite some areas of excellence, particularly in stock trading, Goldman Sachs did not have the prowess of a firm like Salomon Brothers. In 1986 top management determined that this would change.... The management committee believed that in order to expand into new businesses, additional capital ... would be required.

For this reason, at the annual partners meeting held in December, the nine-member management committee for the first time proposed a radical move: taking the firm public through an IPO (initial public offering). If approved, for the first time in 117 years, the firm would be owned by shareholders rather than partners, and partners would morph from partners to employees, albeit very highly compensated employees. For senior partners with many years of service under their belts, the IPO would have meant a staggeringly huge windfall of cash.

For more junior partners, however — especially the new incoming class — an IPO would mean a lesser share in the proceeds as well as a significant drop in the lifetime earnings one would have previously expected from a Goldman partnership — everything they had sweated for over many years.

Venerable Goldman was one of the last major financial institutions to even ponder such a move; virtually all our major competitors had already either merged with other entities or embarked on public sales. (Five years previously, for example, Salomon Brothers had gone public and become Salomon Inc. through a reverse merger with the publicly traded Phibro Corporation, a commodities trading firm.)

As you might guess, most of those who had been partners for a number of years were all for the IPO, which would instantly transform them from very rich men to fabulously rich men, while most new and other less seasoned partners were vehemently opposed. I myself had no strong opinion either way, although I understood the rationale. The fundamental thing was this: you either decided to be like Lazard (which would not go public until 2002) and let the world pass you by, or you decided to be engaged in the world and to understand that the world was changing. Nevertheless, although John Weinberg had agreed to present the majority opinion of the Management Committee to the partners meeting, many in the room felt that he himself was not enthusiastically on board with the notion. Largely due to market conditions, Goldman decided against going public at the time and would not do so until May 1999, by which point I would be long gone.

*   *   *

Ten years before the IPO, in May 1989, the Management Committee agreed to my strong recommendation that we enter the equity investment management business in a major way. I was, in turn, tapped to found and run Goldman's new asset management division. In taking on this new responsibility, I relinquished my role as head of Goldman's equity research department, with Michael Armellino replacing me.

The move was a radical departure for Goldman, which had stayed out of equity management for outside clients because the firm did not want to alienate its institutional customers. But I'd thought for some time that this fear had been overblown. The rest of Wall Street had already thrown caution to the wind. Our announcement followed by barely a week one from Salomon Brothers that they intended to expand their own recently formed asset management group.

As the *New York Times* observed:

> The move represents a significant shift for Goldman … The firm's announcement follows last week's move by Salomon Brothers to expand a recently formed asset management group. Salomon and Goldman had been the only leading Wall Street firms without such divisions. "It really signals a lot," said Michael L. Goldstein, a senior securities analyst at Sanford C. Bernstein Company who follows brokerage firms. Donaldson, Lufkin & Jenrette, Shearson Lehman Hutton and Morgan Stanley have divisions with billions of dollars under management in mutual fund and pension fund accounts. Goldman already has a small index fund operation for pension accounts, but its announcement yesterday signals its desire to gain actively managed stock accounts — the traditional base of the asset management business.

Somewhat ironically, and counterintuitively, Goldman started seeking such accounts at a time of contraction and increased competition in asset management. Many large pension funds were withdrawing assets from the stock market during this period, as their plans matured and they found themselves needing cash to fund retirement benefits. Nevertheless, despite this reality, I remained an optimist: "We're not saying this is nirvana," I told a reporter, "but we think we can get a decent share of the market." The fact of the matter is that I knew we'd be successful in winning asset management accounts because we already had a large base of investment banking relationships with top corporations.

What was our overall strategy? Simply put, we and other Wall Street firms were turning to fee-generating businesses like asset management, where profit margins could be as high as 50 percent, during a period when profits from our traditional business, equity commissions, were down sharply. (Firms that control assets charge their customers an annual fee based on a percentage of the account's size, not a commission.)

It was a huge potential market. And all you needed was a thin sliver to make a profitable business. Very soon after the May announcement, I moved the asset management division out of Goldman's headquarters in lower Manhattan to a separate address in the Wall Street area. I did this mostly for appearances — a signal to institutional customers that the asset management customers would not receive critical research information before customers who were paying high commissions for such services.

* * *

I soon decided that I wanted to start a hedge fund as part of the asset management business, but Goldman management (in the persons of cochairmen Robert E. Rubin and Stephen Friedman) hesitated. They did not want Goldman to be seen as shorting its own investment banking clients. (Ironically, as I write, just about all that Goldman sells its clients are premium-fee hedge fund products.)

Despite Goldman's reticence, I remained intrigued and excited about the hedge fund model. In large part because of this, by late spring 1991, after twenty-five years with Goldman, I'd decided it was time for me to leave the firm and start my own concern. I told Rubin and Friedman, who tried to talk me out of it and offered to put me on the executive committee. But my wife said to me, "How old do you have to be, and how rich do you have to be, before you do what you want to do?" In the end, the firm and I agreed on a departure date of November 29, of which I informed the *New York Times*:

> "The nub of the story is that for the past two years, I've been wearing three hats, and three were just too many," Mr. Cooperman said yesterday. "The proof of the pudding is that when I announced I was retiring, they said, 'Fine, but just find two people to replace you.' I decided it was time to narrow my focus."
>
> Mr. Cooperman will devote his time to what he says he loves most and has been most successful at: managing money. He plans to set up his own small investment partnership, with fewer than 100 participants and between $200 million and $300 million in assets, in which he will be a major investor. "This has been a dream all my adult life," he said.

My separation from Goldman was not complete. We remained on the best of terms, and to this day I treasure the memory of my experience there and the friends I made at the firm. Even though I've made the largest part of my fortune post-Goldman, the truth is that I arrived at Goldman with nothing but debt and departed Goldman a very wealthy man. And Goldman and I continued a business connection. I agreed that I'd consult for the GS Capital Growth Fund, a $475 million mutual fund that I had managed since its launch in April 1990. I also agreed to use Goldman as the prime broker for my new business. In addition, Goldman wound up investing with me. Before I left, I told Goldman, "I'm not leaving over money; I'm very happy at the firm. If my having my own hedge fund is a violation of my noncompete, I'll just sit in a friend's office and manage my own money."

But they said, "Not at all. We don't want to have a hedge fund, so you can do what you want to do."

As might be expected, my retirement triggered some significant rearrangement within the asset management unit at Goldman, with a clearer division between the business management and the investment decision-making. I handed the job of chairman and chief executive of the unit to Michael R. Armellino, who agreed to return after retiring several months before from my old job as director of research for the parent firm. The senior money manager at the unit, James S. McClure, was now to report to Armellino.

It is worth noting that the expanded asset management unit was just a little over two years old when I decided to depart. I'd run it throughout that period, and in that brief time it had grown to encompass 154 employees, nine investment products, and some $28 billion under management. I was (and remain) very proud of my work there, and I was gratified and grateful when, in a memo announcing my departure, Rubin and Friedman voiced praise: "Lee has worked tirelessly and epitomized the best of Goldman Sachs, putting the firm's interests above his own."

A degree of sentimentality made it hard for me to leave Goldman. It was where I had first "made my bones" and that had given me the best opportunity to launch my career in high finance. But just like a bird eventually leaves the nest, my departure was not only necessary but inevitable. I needed a new mountain to climb, a new frontier to explore. And I was eager to begin.

PART III

OMEGA YEARS

CHAPTER 6

OMEGA – LEADING BY EXAMPLE

Example is leadership.

— ALBERT SCHWEITZER

In his fabulous 2009 book *Born to Run*, author Christopher McDougall tells the story of how every morning in Africa, a gazelle wakes up knowing that it must outrun the fastest lion, or it will be killed and eaten. Also, every morning in Africa, a lion wakes up knowing that it must outrun the slowest gazelle, or it will starve. As McDougall points out, "It doesn't matter whether you're the lion or a gazelle — when the sun comes up, you'd better be running." It has been with this same mentality that I've pursued my career and, most especially, my time running my investment firm Omega Advisors.

After a period of preparation, I launched the private investment partnership Omega Advisors in December 1991. We started with several hundred million dollars under management. At our peak, during the first half of 2014, AUM was over $10 billion.

This is not to say that I didn't make mistakes along the way. In fact, I've often said that my mistakes, if brought together, could be paraded up Fifth Avenue five abreast. I've also said, and firmly believe, that anyone in this business who says they haven't made mistakes either doesn't make decisions or is a liar. Of course, I, like everyone else, have had "down" years. Typically, a would-be client would sit me down and ask, "Lee, what am I going to earn if I invest with you?" I would always answer: "I can't tell you exactly what you are going to earn, but let me tell you what makes me happy and what doesn't make me happy. Because if what makes me happy doesn't make you happy, then that is the basis for a flawed relationship, and I'd rather you not invest."

My objectives in my fund were straightforward enough. As a long/short hedge fund, I could, of course, be "net short" (a bearish bet) or "net flat" (out of the market) whenever I felt it necessary, even though I preferred to be "net long" (a bullish bet). If I lost money either long or short, that would mean I got it wrong, and I would *not* be happy about that. Secondly, I liked to beat the S&P 500 (after performance fees). I didn't want to walk into a client meeting having underperformed some mindless benchmark, even though I might still be making a lot of money for both myself and my client. I'd also remind the potential client that I didn't run a highly leveraged portfolio, so, in general (the S&P 500 "bogey" aside), 10–12 percent average annual returns after fees made me happy. Finally, I liked having less volatility than the market. So long as a potential investor was comfortable with these assumptions and aligned with them, I was generally happy to take them on board.

By the time I closed the firm as a client-facing hedge fund and converted Omega into a family office, our average annualized return over the life of the firm was approximately 13 percent (net of fees), four hundred basis points (net of fees) above the S&P 500. During that time, we were on average 70 percent net long, with next-to-no leverage. All in all, that added up to a pretty good track record. Investors paying very high fees for the management of their assets deserve superior results. Over the long haul, that's exactly what our investors at Omega got.

The title of this book is not *How to Make Billions Managing a Hedge Fund*. However, I think it will be useful to provide a brief snapshot of our processes and philosophy at Omega.

In general, the bulk of our assets tended to be in the United States. However, we also invested in some developed-economy markets in Europe and elsewhere.

Overall, our strategy was to seek 15 percent per annum lumpy returns, rather than 8–10 percent per annum straight-line returns. We were willing to take equity-like risk in pursuit of equity-like returns and to deal with *some* market volatility in pursuit of those returns. Our goal was always to exceed returns on the S&P 500 by several hundred basis points per annum, net of fees. General partners had a large share of our assets under management, so their interests were aligned with those of our investing partners. At the outset, I was the only general partner *per se*, although more were, of course, to come in. However, I considered all employees to be partners in a sense. If someone is worth having on staff, then that someone is worth compensating well, which became the standard at Omega just as it always had been at Goldman.

Somewhat unique in the hedge fund industry were our equal focuses on both top-down macro analysis and bottom-up stock picking, a powerful combination. This set an investment landscape

> Investors paying very high fees for the management of their assets deserve superior results.

for Omega that allowed us to have a view, for example, of where the aggregate equity market should trade in a given year. That view would, as you'd expect, depend on our assessment of economic activity both within and outside the US, our assessment of earnings growth, our assessment of monetary and fiscal policies, and our assessment and evaluation of supply and demand for equities, all of which helped inform us as to what exposure we wanted in our portfolio at any given time.

In turn, that knowledge helped us digest what the analysts brought to us in the way of recommendations. In essence, the macroeconomic and risk-market outlooks gave us a better grasp of implications for relative sector performance. While we always remained bottom-up stock pickers and didn't target sector weightings *per se*, we could nevertheless, with a macro outlook, lean toward (or away from) given sectors based upon that outlook and its forward-looking implications.

For example, if the outlook was for a below-average period of economic growth with low inflation, we would want to emphasize those companies that were somewhat insulated from the economic cycle, particularly those insulated from competition and capable of growing independently from the economic cycle. This approach can lead you to certain sectors, whether those be technology, healthcare, or so on.

Our position sizing was always a function of several input variables. One was liquidity. We never wanted to be so large in a security that we couldn't get out without disturbing the market price in a significant way. Secondly, and perhaps most importantly, we would look quite carefully at the risk/reward set that an analyst presented to our Stock Selection Committee. The analysts would always give us an upside target and an assessment of the downside risk. Then there

would be extensive discussion of the name, the fundamentals supporting the recommendation, and the risks surrounding it. But the core
of the discussion was always the analyst's judgment as to upside and
downside. The more significant the ratio of upside return to downside
risk, the more inclined we would be to take on a sizeable position,
adjusting for liquidity.

Those were the two principal metrics that we would look at in
choosing and sizing a given name. Typically, at Omega, a large *long*
position would be 3–5 percent of the asset base, and a large *short*
position would be 1–2 percent of the asset base.

The best circumstance under which to exit a name was, of course,
if it had met all of what we expected of it in terms of fundamentals
and those fundamentals were reflected in the stock price. If it met
our stock price target, we exited because the name no longer had the
upside potential that was there when we entered the position. The
less pleasant way to exit was to realize we were simply wrong on our
assessment of fundamentals – in other words, because the name was
not delivering as we had anticipated when we initiated the position.
A third catalyst for exiting, not as satisfying as the first but sometimes
good enough, was when a given name might have been doing well
and meeting the fundamental assessment we had at the outset, but
where the analyst had found another name within the same sector that
they considered even more attractive. In that case, we would exchange
good fundamentals for even better fundamentals. We would also sell
if our overall market outlook changed in such a manner as to make
us want to raise cash.

In broad strokes, the principles and procedures described above
were what made Omega tick as successfully as it did.

* * *

Of course, the hedge fund concept was nothing new when I entered the field. Its roots went back an entire generation. Following a career as a sociologist and a writer for *Fortune*, Alfred W. Jones started a limited partnership, A.W. Jones & Co., in 1952, and a second one, A.W. Jones Associates, in 1961. By that time, Jones had gained quite a fanbase among his investors for having compounded their money over nine years at an annualized rate of 21 percent. Jones had no competition in the hedge fund field until 1964, when one of his general partners broke away and started his own fund, with other general partners to follow his example in due course. And from there, of course, the hedge fund industry grew at high speed — albeit with some bumps along the road, not the least of which was the bear market of 2008–2009.

Throughout 2007, I remained bullish about 2008. In December, I told an interviewer on CNN: "I'm still constructive on stocks for 2008, for now, holding aside the potential effects of the 2008 presidential election. While there is certainly a fair amount to worry about — subprime and housing issues, bank write-offs against capital, a slowing economy and slowing earnings — there are several reasons to be bullish on stocks.

"First, market valuations are very attractive relative to government bond yields, and the S&P is priced today akin to previous market trough. The market has already discounted an awful lot of the negative news. Second, I expect the US economy can escape recession in 2008. Housing weakness should be partly offset by more significant inventory build-up, and housing's effect on the US economy should moderate in the second half of 2008. Employment data doesn't foreshadow recession either. Leading indicators of the labor market point to positive growth in monthly payrolls. Before a recession, average monthly payrolls drop about five-hundred thousand a month. We're currently growing monthly payrolls by about one-hundred thousand a month.

"Third, core consumer inflation and inflation expectations are tame and within the Federal Reserve's comfort zone. With tame inflation and a dislocated market that is still not functioning properly, this should allow the Fed to cut interest rates and inject liquidity into the system. Fourth, earnings and dividends should increase in 2008. Bear markets in the US are usually preceded by an overheating economy, accelerated inflation, tight money, and bad valuations. None of these, in our view, are present today."

In other words, like most others on Wall Street, I didn't see the realities of 2008 coming.

Of course, all this was joined at the hip with the banking crisis. We at Omega totally misunderstood the significance of the Lehman insolvency (September 2008) and its impact on the economy, and we weren't alone. The US government, and indeed most people, didn't understand it. The surprise with respect to Lehman was the reach it had into so many other financial institutions and the freezing of credit that it brought about. The recession we experienced in 2008 and the first half of 2009 would not have been nearly as severe without the freezing of credit flows between financial intermediaries because of the Lehman insolvency.

There are always low moments, but there are also always opportunities on the horizon. You come through things.

The bear market of 2008 to early 2009 was devastating to Omega as well as to just about everyone else on the Street. I lost a lot of money for my investors. I felt worse for the investors than I did for myself. I was the largest investor in the fund, so I lost more money than anybody else.

But I felt I'd let down those who'd had faith in me. The good news is we came roaring back during the last six months of 2009. We held our positions, and we prospered in the long run.

There are always low moments, but there are also always opportunities on the horizon. You come through things. I'd previously had a big problem in 1998, which will be the topic of the next chapter. And I would once again be navigating troubled waters in 2015–2017, as will be the topic two chapters on. Nevertheless, I'm very, very proud of what we accomplished at Omega over the years.

The not-so-secret ingredient has been our people. I've often compared myself to the conductor of an orchestra. The conductor is key, but without the orchestra he is nothing — just a pointless jerk standing alone in the spotlight, waving a baton, and looking foolish. Over the decades, I've had some truly great and very smart people with me both as partners and as employees. Without them, Omega would have been nothing. But as any of them can tell you, I'm a conductor who has insisted that his musicians work hard and perform well. That said, I have never in my career asked anyone to work harder than I've been willing to work myself. In this way, I've made a point of leading by example.

By far, the most valuable colleague I had at Omega was Steve Einhorn, of whom I've previously spoken regarding his role working with me at Goldman. Steve joined Omega upon his retirement from Goldman in 1999, and thereafter we were joined at the hip. As Lawrence C. Strauss of *Barron's* wrote in 2013:

> While Cooperman, 70, and Einhorn, 64, don't finish each other's sentences, they think enough alike to finish each other's paragraphs. Says Einhorn: "Lee has an ability to isolate the critical variables that will

ultimately determine the direction of a stock price before many others do."

Cooperman returns the compliment, lauding Einhorn's smarts and judgment, and calling him "a man of integrity who cares about the clients of the firm and me. What more can one ask of a partner?"

To this day, long after my conversion of Omega to a family office, Steve and I remain the closest of friends. Looking back over my entire career in investing, and the many talented, honorable, and valuable associates I've worked with along the way, Steve ranks in the very top-most tier.

CHAPTER 7

DECEPTION – CLAYTON LEWIS AND THE AZERBAIJAN FIASCO

Tricks and treachery are the practice of fools that
don't have brains enough to be honest.

— BENJAMIN FRANKLIN

My all-time worst investment was the result of subterfuge by an employee whom I trusted, respected, and believed to be an honorable man. I am normally a pretty good judge of character, but in this case, I got it wrong.

I hired Clayton Lewis out of Goldman Sachs in 1995 with a $225,000 minimum guarantee (salary and bonus); that year, I paid him over $1,125,000 all in. The following two years (1996 and 1997), he did an outstanding job, with a focus on emerging markets, and I paid him over $28 million combined. He complained about his remuneration in 1996 (almost $17 million). In retrospect, I probably should have taken this as a red flag, a sign of whom I was dealing with. Keep in mind, I was also paying his entire staff of five people. I told him over lunch at my country club that if he felt that he was undercompensated, I'd pay him his bonus and he could leave. After that, I'd just stay away from emerging markets, a sector in which I had no personal expertise and in which I was not particularly interested. He emphatically declined my offer. I wish he'd said yes, because he then proceeded, in 1998, to lose everything he'd made for the firm in 1995, 1996, and 1997.

Two years later, in 1998, Lewis became aware of what turned out to be a highly illegal and completely unethical plot to collude with corrupt Azerbaijani officials to gain control of SOCAR (the State Oil Company of the Azerbaijan Republic), the giant government-owned oil company. SOCAR boasted some seventy-five thousand Azerbaijani employees and represented the most valuable and important asset of any kind in that entire country.

A key player in the plan to takeover SOCAR was Czech-born Viktor Kožen, whom *Fortune* magazine subsequently dubbed "the Pirate of Prague" because of shady dealings in his homeland. Given his history, and unbeknownst to the majority of those who eventually invested in his enterprise, Kožen was evidently a man who could feel quite at home in what we eventually learned to be the generally corrupt business world of Azerbaijan. Separated only seven years earlier from the collapsed Soviet Union, Azerbaijan was at that time a place of fledgling, Wild West capitalism where virtually everything was for sale, including "justice" and governmental influence.

In this case, Kožen had made clandestine financial arrangements with Azerbaijani government officials, which ostensibly incentivized them to privatize SOCAR, beginning with the distribution of privatization vouchers among the citizenry that would serve as *de facto* options on discounted shares of SOCAR. Koženýʼs scheme called for him to buy enough of those vouchers so that immediately upon the presumed privatization of SOCAR, he and his conglomerate of investors would be able to acquire enough shares to take control of SOCAR at a bargain-basement price.

Then as now, the economy of Azerbaijan was defined by oil. As *Fortune* magazine noted:

> Azerbaijan has always been about oil. You can even smell it as you drive into Baku, cooking in the rusting refinery outside town, oozing from decrepit wells into black inland pools. Smaller than Indiana, sandwiched between Russia and Iran, Azerbaijan was the world's first big oil producer, generating more than half the globe's supply by 1900. Under Soviet control, the sprawling Azeri oil industry grew antiquated and inefficient. But by 1997, after President Heydar Aliyev, a 74-year-old former KGB general and Soviet Politburo member, had stabilized the country, Azerbaijan was enjoying a new oil boom.[3]

Although Clayton Lewis was fully briefed on the illicit aspects of the proposed SOCAR acquisition, he made absolutely no mention of these facts in his representations to the Omega investment committee or to other investors. Had he done so, Omega never would have gone anywhere near the project, and Lewis knew it. But we were lied to by Lewis.

---

3   Peter Elkind, "The Incredible Half-Billion-Dollar Azerbaijani Oil Swindle," *Fortune*, March 6, 2000.

Based on Lewis's representations, Omega invested $110 million of client money in the project. Partners added $15 million from their own investment pool, with two-thirds of that amount coming out of my own resources. Lewis also, on his own, gathered investments from several additional sources: $15 million from Columbia University, $15 million from American International Group (AIG), and $25 million from a cadre of smaller investors. (For example, former Senate majority leader George Mitchell put in $200,000 and signed on to the board of a Koženy venture associated with the enterprise, Oily Rock Group, Ltd.)

Given his knowledge at the time, Lewis made a fateful decision to induce our firm and fellow investors into a deal that was tainted with corruption from the start. This he formally admitted, under oath, before a federal judge in February 2004 when pleading guilty to having violated the Foreign Corrupt Practices Act (FCPA). Six years later, in May 2010, he wrote a letter to me in which he further elucidated his behavior:

> ... I did not raise Koženy's financial relationship [with Azerbaijani government officials] in the due diligence memorandum or in the two investment approval meetings where the investment was presented to relevant Omega personnel, including yourself.... I failed in my responsibilities to you and to Omega ... Omega did not authorize Koženy's conduct in any manner, and I take full responsibility for my failures and for the terrible misjudgment of recommending that Omega pursue an investment associated with Viktor Koženy.

To make a long story short, Koženy's surreptitious scheme to use back-channel influence to gain control of SOCAR did not work. Whatever his arrangements with Azerbaijani officials, those officials reneged on those arrangements, and the privatization did not occur at that time. According to the FBI agent who eventually headed the investigation into this affair, "It appears the corrupt Azeri officials scammed the scammers. They pocketed the bribe money without ever delivering the quid pro quo."

Koženy, in turn, stiffed his investors by not returning the balances of their funds that had not yet been used to buy vouchers. As well, it subsequently came out that Koženy himself had already made a fortune by selling privatization vouchers to his investors for far more money that he had paid to acquire them, despite covenants in the investment documents prohibiting him from doing so. (Koženy's cost was less than a dollar per voucher, while he charged his investors $25 per voucher.) Of all the money that the investors had given Koženy, only about $11 million had been used to bribe Azerbaijani officials. Most of the balance wound up with Koženy.

Koženy was wily enough to be in the Bahamas when, in 2003, based on a complaint made by Omega after Lewis had left the firm and we had come to realize the broader picture, he was indicted by Manhattan District Attorney Robert Morgenthau for swindling Omega and other investors. Among the media that took note of his indictment was the student newspaper of his own alma mater, *The Harvard Crimson*:

> Koženy was charged with 15 counts of grand larceny and two counts of criminal possession of stolen property, for allegedly stealing from investment funds managed by Manhattan-based Omega Advisors,

Manhattan District Attorney Robert M. Morgenthau
announced.... Kožen, who received his bachelor's
degree in economics from Harvard, could face up to
25 years in prison if convicted.

Two years later, in 2005, Kožený was indicted on twenty-seven counts of bribery in US District Court in Manhattan under the FCPA. However, in 2010, a Bahamian court rejected a US bid for his extradition. As I write today, in 2023, Kožený remains a fugitive from American justice.

Several of his other cohorts were not so lucky. Clayton Lewis was to plead guilty in February 2004. More indictments came down in October 2005. These included David Pinkerton, a managing director of the Global Investment Company, a subsidiary of AIG, and Frederic Bourke Jr., head of a private consortium that invested some $8 million in the venture.

Bourke received a federal prison sentence of a year and a day, plus a $1 million fine, for his knowledge of and cooperation in Kožený's scheme. Pinkerton was eventually cleared of any knowledge of the plot, and the Justice Department dropped charges against him. Kožený's associate Tom Farrell, who led most of the operations on the ground in Azerbaijan, was also charged in the matter and, like Clayton Lewis, cooperated with the government early on to minimize his pending sentence.

Charges were never filed against Omega or me, although, despite our proactive, complete, and willing cooperation in the investigation, we were eventually fined $500,000 for our alleged negligence in failing to detect Lewis's lies sooner than we did. To this day, I remain bitter that the government knew that Omega was one of the swindled, not the swindlers, but didn't care, as the prosecutors wanted another notch in their belt. When that fine was levied, in July 2007, I wrote a letter to our investors informing them that the "saga relating to Omega's 1998 investment in the privatization program in Azerbaijan has come to an end. We were shocked and dismayed at Lewis's betrayal of the trust placed in him." Commenting to Reuters on Omega's settlement with investigators and prosecutors, Omega's lawyer Robert Anello said, "I am happy that the government has understood that Omega has acted appropriately since it learned of Mr. Lewis's improper conduct."

True to form, Clayton Lewis continued to lie even during his "cooperation" with authorities, perjuring himself on the witness stand in a New York grand jury proceeding associated with the case. None-theless, when he was finally sentenced in the spring of 2013, the result was (and there is no other word) absurd. Lewis received a sentence of time served (six days) and a $100 fine. (By comparison, $100 is the fine that one who has parked illegally in Manhattan pays after being towed.) In response to all this, I felt compelled to write a letter of protest to the sentencing judge:

April 9th, 2013

Honorable Naomi Reice Buchwald
United States District Judge
Southern District of New York
500 Pearl Street
New York NY 10007–1312
Re: U.S. v Clayton Lewis
03–CR–00930–NRB

Dear Judge Buchwald:

With respect for your reputation as an outstanding jurist, I feel compelled to write this letter to express my profound disappointment with the sentence you recently handed down in the captioned case. Six days' time-served and a one-hundred-dollar fine strikes this observer, for one, as an outrageous travesty of justice.

Had the government solicited a victim impact statement from me, I would have reminded them of the following:

- Mr. Lewis knowingly lured my firm, Omega Advisors Inc., into a deal tainted by his and other's corruption, occasioning the loss of well over $100 million by my firm's clients and employees.
- He lied repeatedly about his activities to me, his partners, and colleagues, and to several of my firm's biggest clients whom he solicited personally for the tainted investment.
- He pleaded guilty to having perjured himself before a New York State Grand Jury.
- He withdrew his sworn testimony in a related civil case in the United Kingdom, acknowledging that he had lied.
- He was considered so compromised as a witness that he was never called to testify in the one related criminal case (against Frederic Bourke) that went to trial.
- As a direct result of his bad acts, I spent $14 million, personally and on behalf of my firm's clients, in defending against baseless claims of complicity in his wrongdoing and in providing witnesses and information requested by the government.

When prosecutors exercise their discretion in a manner contrary to the interests of a defendant, they open themselves to a possible charge of abuse of prosecutorial discretion. But it seems that if they act in a manner congruent with the defendant's interests, there is no avenue for challenging their actions, even if in doing so they run roughshod over the countervailing interests of those the defendant wronged. In such a situation, it is left to the presiding judge to ensure that justice is done, even if that means, as it sometimes does, exceeding the government sentencing recommendation. In this case, you failed to discharge that public trust.

I suspect that I understand what happened here. Some of Mr. Lewis's crimes occurred 15 years ago, and it would be only natural for a degree of prosecutorial, and perhaps judicial, fatigue to have set in — one reason that a victim impact statement should have been solicited to remind the government and the court of what took place. Mr. Lewis has expressed contrition for his actions, though (as the record reflects) he is a gifted dissembler, and whether he regrets the deed or only getting caught is at least an open question. In the nine years since his 2004 guilty plea, Mr. Lewis has reportedly assisted the government in building cases against Mr. Kožený and others and stood ready and willing to testify at trial — even if, as an admitted serial liar, his credibility as a witness was considered too compromised to call him to do so in the one case (against Frederic Bourke) that got that far. Undoubtedly, some consideration should justifiably have been given for Mr. Lewis's cooperation. But letting him off with a nugatory wrist-slap is an insult to the broader public interest.

I know that the horse has left the corral on this and that nothing I can say will reopen the matter. But I would ask you to reflect on whether the purposes and goals of the criminal sanction were well served by your decision here. In a growing number of financial sector civil cases, federal judges are rejecting government endorsed deals and settlements as being too lenient. Had you approached even the financial aspect of Mr. Lewis's sentencing with a similar measure of skepticism (cf. the related case of *U.S. v. Bodmer*, where one month earlier a Swiss citizen, whose conduct unlike Lewis's was lawful in his own country and who unlike Lewis actually testified for the government at trial, was sentenced by Judge Scheindlin to time served and a $500,000 fine), it might have sent a cautionary message to other would be crooks in the future.

This result is especially galling in that Omega, as the principal victim here, proactively approached the government (both the US attorney's office and the Manhattan district attorney's office) to expose the wrongdoing in this case, cooperated extensively with prosecutors in illuminating what took place, and was then assessed a $500,000 fine for purportedly failing to detect Mr. Lewis's wrongdoing (which by its nature was intended to deceive) sooner. Yet, as a result of your decision, Mr. Lewis was fined 0.02% of what Omega was fined. That is something straight out of *Through the Looking-Glass*!

The government is for good reason never the final arbiter of what justice demands — the court is. In the case of *U.S. v. Clayton Lewis*, by acceding to prosecutors' self-serving sentencing recommendation, you dealt that bedrock principle a blow.

Respectfully,
Leon G. Cooperman

I never received a response from Judge Buchwald, and I suppose I never should have expected to. The entire episode, played out over a period of years, was one of the saddest and most grueling of my entire professional career, with my investors and me losing a great deal of money and my firm losing a great deal of prestige.

It is interesting to see the extent of damage that can be done by just one rogue employee who makes an art of deception, duplicity, and betrayal of a trust bestowed in good faith. For my part, my chief regret about this matter is the damage it did to the investments entrusted to me by my clients and partners. That we were able to recoup at least some of our investment through the settlement of a suit against Kožený in the High Court of Justice in London in 2009 gave little satisfaction.

There's an old saying: "Those who don't know the value of loyalty can never appreciate the cost of betrayal." I certainly know the value of loyalty, just as I now, sadly, know the cost of betrayal. By this I do not simply mean the monetary cost but the cost of faith in others, the cost of reputation, and the cost of dignity. But one soldiers on. There's always another chapter to be written.

CHAPTER 8

THE OPERA AIN'T OVER TILL THE FAT LADY SINGS

*Someone is sitting in the shade today because
someone planted a tree a long time ago.*

— WARREN BUFFETT

On September 21, 2016, the Securities and Exchange Commission charged my firm, Omega Advisors, and me personally with insider trading. The SEC alleged that, in July 2010, I had generated about $6 million in profits by purchasing stock and bonds, and trading in call options, of Atlas Pipeline Partners (APL), in which we'd already had stock and bond positions since years earlier) in advance of the sale of that firm's natural gas–processing facility in Elk City, Oklahoma — a deal about which I supposedly had privileged, prior knowledge. (Those stock and bond gains existed only on paper; ironically, they'd evaporated by the time we exited those positions long after the deal's announcement, having held on to them far too long because I had a fundamental, if ultimately wrong, belief in APL's prospects.)

The possibility of such charges had been in the wind for many months. As reported in the *New York Times* and other media at the time, the SEC had issued a Wells Notice to Omega the previous March, notifying us of a likely enforcement action. And one year before that, in March 2015, the Commission had issued broad subpoenas to Omega and me for records (and later, for my testimony) relevant to the transactions in question.

When the first subpoenas were issued, I promptly offered, through our lawyers (Dan Kramer and Ted Wells of Paul, Weiss, Rifkind, Wharton & Garrison LLP), that if the subpoenas were withdrawn (removing, at least temporarily, the cloud over my business that they'd created), I would meet voluntarily with the Commission staff and attempt to address all their questions about the trading at issue, saying that the subpoenas could always be reinstated if I could not satisfy the staff that I had done nothing wrong. In that context, I would have voluntarily tolled all relevant statutes of limitations so that the government's claims regarding APL, in particular, would not be "time-barred" in the interim.

The SEC staff flat out refused, and we commenced the voluminous document production required by the subpoena — in the process, running up millions of dollars in (what would, in the case of a smaller firm, have been crippling) legal and data-warehousing costs. That "rolling production" process was substantially completed by the end of 2015, and the Wells Notice came in mid-March of the following year.

Six months later, at a September 2016 meeting which we had requested, the SEC's director of enforcement, Andrew Ceresney, advised our attorneys that the SEC would not agree to settle without a five-year industry bar, which he must have realized would have been tantamount to an admission of wrongdoing, effectively ending my otherwise spotless fifty-year career on Wall Street in disgrace. That was a nonstarter for me, and I rejected their offer.

Upon receiving my decision, the SEC promptly filed suit, alleging, *inter alia*, that we had traded in the securities of APL based on material, nonpublic information. On the same day the charges were filed, I had a conference call with investors on which I informed them that I had refused to settle and intended to fight. The *New York Times* reported, "The stage is set for what is expected to be a no-holds-barred legal battle between a gruff, outspoken investor and an agency that has come under criticism for not taking more cases to trial."

Our firm had been operating under a cloud and experiencing capital outflows ever since the highly publicized issuance of the subpoenas in March 2015. Now, with the filing of formal charges, those capital outflows accelerated through the end of 2016 and into May 2017, when a settlement was reached — essentially, the same deal to which I would have agreed the previous September had it been on the table. Instead, we had to go through the needless expenditure by both sides of financial and human resources of substantial magnitude, only to arrive back at what I'd been willing to sign on to many months before.

Even after announcing the terms of the settlement — which included no industry (or officer-and-director) suspension or bar, no admission of wrongdoing, a financial payment that was roughly half the government's original ask, an obey-the-law injunction, and various compliance enhancements — Omega continued to bleed assets, due, in large part, to the pall cast on us by the government's unproven allegations. It seemed that such damage, once inflicted, cannot be undone. I must laugh grimly when people tell me that I "won" — two years of my life and many millions of dollars in legal expenses later, with my business in shambles, it was a Pyrrhic victory, if any.

Nowhere have I made a categorical statement that the SEC's charges were spurious. My consent agreement with the SEC, like virtually all other such SEC agreements, includes a "no admit/no deny" gag clause that prohibits me from doing so. I wish this were not the case. What I can say is that I found the Commission's conduct throughout the process abusive and coercive, relying on rank intimidation to wrestle settlements from targets whose only other choice is ruinous litigation.

Interestingly, most enforcement cases brought by the SEC ultimately settle without going to trial. In the decades since the issuance of the no admit/no deny gag rule in 1972, the SEC has settled thousands of cases with judgments containing those provisions.

Not a few informed observers have, over the years, pointed out that this policy seems inappropriate. Although never found guilty of anything, much less convicted of a crime, an individual or firm is nonetheless enjoined from defending their name and reputation in public. Many believe that the SEC's practice places unconstitutional restraints on First Amendment rights.

Settlements are often the result of a defendant simply deciding on the most cost-effective way of getting on with their business and their life. As I've described, a firm can easily spend millions of dollars simply responding to SEC subpoenas. To then contemplate a lengthy and expensive trial — even if one were confident of an eventual vindication — is, for most, too daunting from both a financial and professional perspective.

Therefore, many defendants caught in the government's crosshairs, even those unjustly accused, seek to settle in order to save both money and time and to put the matter behind them. Their reputation ends up besmirched, justifiably or not, in a manner that prohibits any public attempt at self-defense after the fact. The only ones who come

PHOTOGRAPHS

Me (standing) at play in The Bronx, probably around 1951.

My Hunter College graduation photo, 1964.

Wedding Bells, 1964.

Wedding Bells, 1964.

My Columbia Business School graduation photo, 1967.

An appearance on Louis Rukeyser's Wall Street Week, *mid-1982.*

Strategy

WARREN E. BUFFETT

Investment Strategy Highlights

The Market Balance Sheet
Deleveraging of the Corporate Sector

Leon G. Cooperman
Steven G. Einhorn
July/August 1982

Warren Buffett's 1982 note to me after reading my 1982 Business Week *letter concerning Dr. Henry Singleton and Teledyne, which I have hanging on my office wall: "I always enjoy both the quality of your writing and the quality of your thinking. Your letter to* Business Week *regarding Teledyne was 100 percent on the mark."*

With my longtime friend and colleague, Steve Einhorn.

A fishing weekend with my brother Howard, at right.

Left to right: Daughter-in-law Jodi, son Wayne, Me, Toby,
granddaughter Kyra, grandson Asher, granddaughter Courtney,
son Michael, and daughter-in-law Anne.

Granddaughter Courtney with Toby, Short Hills, New Jersey, 2018.

*Left to right: Me (standing), Diana Cooperman (sitting),
daughter-in-law Anne (standing), son Michael (standing),
brother Howard (sitting), Toby (standing), grandson Asher (standing),
and nephew Jay, who is Howard's son and Diana's husband (sitting).*

*Left to right: Son Wayne, Me, granddaughter Courtney, Toby,
granddaughter Kyra, and daughter-in-law Jodi – Bahamas, 2010.*

Grandchildren Courtney, Asher, and Kyra – 2012.

Toby and I meet with each new class of the Cooperman College Scholars.
This is the class of 2020

out ahead are the bureaucrats at the SEC. No matter how weak their evidence or reasoning might have been at the time charges were filed, they still get a notch in their belts. Protected in most cases by sovereign immunity, the government pays no price when it overreaches.

Ironically, the SEC policy seems, to me and others, to fly in the face of one of the Commission's key stated goals: to assure the market the benefits of full transparency and disclosure. How does a gag order align with this goal?

There have been several attempted court challenges to no admit/ no deny settlements in recent memory, none of which have proved successful. One hopes that the prevailing winds will shift in due course. Perhaps then I can have my say.

* * *

During the summer of 2018, not long after turning seventy-five years of age, I made a decision that I suppose I'd been putting off for a while and announced a major change for Omega. That's when I sent out the following letter:

July 23, 2018

Dear Fellow Investor,

It is with mixed emotions that I write to inform you of my decision to convert Omega to a family office at year-end, which will necessitate redeeming all outside capital at that time. This decision is a very personal one driven not by any health concerns, but solely by how I want to spend my remaining years.

I turned 75 last April. It is my understanding that if you make it past 65 and cancer doesn't get you, you can expect to live on average to 85. Hopefully, I can improve on that average, but in any event, I don't want to spend the rest of my life chasing the S&P 500 and focused on generating returns on investor capital. This view was reinforced when I attended a Kenny Rogers concert this past winter. Mr. Rogers, best known for his signature song "The Gambler" ("You've got to know when to hold 'em, know when to fold 'em"), clearly doesn't follow his own advice. He had great difficulty in getting around the stage and acknowledged that at almost 80, he shouldn't be performing any longer, but that he'd been divorced four times and needed the money! Well, I've been happily married to the same woman for 54 years, don't need the money, and know when to fold 'em. As many of you know, I have taken the Giving Pledge, and my financial wealth is earmarked to be returned to society in the hope of benefitting those in need, prominent among them youngsters who can use a helping hand in their quest to achieve the American Dream as I have.

I am pleased that at present, given the firm's positive performance over the past two-and-a-half years, all of you are at a record high on your investments, which is important to me as I plan this next move. I am also pleased that our vice chairman, Steve Einhorn, and I will be consulting with each other in our respective family offices, continuing a personal and professional relationship that spans 45 years.

Although I will be withdrawing from managing other people's money at year-end, I will remain active in the financial markets managing my own. If I can ever be of informal assistance to you as a sounding board, please know that you can always reach out and ask. I know that Steve feels the same.

I am also pleased that Omega Credit Opportunities Fund, under the able direction of Sam Martini and Eric Schneider, will continue (under a new name), and that Rebecca Pacholder (an Omega portfolio manager for the past six years) will be launching a new fund focused on high-yield debt and distressed securities. I wish them each the best of luck and, through my family office, I will be a substantial investor in both.

Between now and year-end, we will be focused on trying to grow your capital. Since more than half of our AUM is General Partner capital, our interests continue to be aligned with yours.

From the bottom of my heart, I thank you all for your many years of support.

Sincerely,
Leon G. Cooperman

There comes a time when every major league player must hang up his glove and make way for newer, younger, more energetic players. That's just the way of things. Nevertheless, I'd be lying if I said I believed in the concept of retirement — at least, for myself. Richard Branson has said that he doesn't think retirement should be the goal of life. "Instead," he has commented, "I think *happiness* should be. I've never thought [of] work as work or play; to me, it's all living and learning. The way I see it, life is all about striving and growing. I never want to have made it; I want to continue making it."

Yes, yes — I know. In my retirement letter to Omega's investors, I said, "I don't want to spend the rest of my life chasing the S&P 500 and focused on generating returns on investor capital." But perhaps that sentence is just evidence of why one should try to avoid speaking in absolutes.

> There comes a time when every major league player must hang up his glove and make way for newer, younger, more energetic players. That's just the way of things.

I often tell young people that the way to be successful is to "do what you love and love what you do." If you love what you do, you will never, in a sense, "work" a day in your life. But at the same time, you'll be bound to get damn good at whatever it is you choose to do. This applies as much to architects, computer programmers, carpenters, detectives, athletes, physicians, and teachers as it does to Wall Street investment managers.

At the end of the day, it is simply not in my nature to be idle. In the time since the end of 2018, I have kept myself extremely busy on two fronts. First, continuing to manage my own (and my family's) investments through the Omega Family Office. I do this with the same vigor and attention to detail that I've always brought to such activities. Second, I am deeply involved in orchestrating and executing the complex process of giving away my personal fortune to organizations and institutions worthy of support.

This second task is a complex one and takes up much of my time. John D. Rockefeller once said, "Giving should be entered into in just the same way as investing. Giving *is* investing." And investing takes homework. But I've always loved the homework of investing, and that hasn't changed. And the homework of philanthropy is a joyous task. It allows me to spend my old age planting seeds for the future. And that is truly gratifying.

In short, I've still got a more-than-full schedule. I thoroughly enjoy what I am doing, just as I always have. And I plan on keeping it up for as long as I possibly can. As the old saying goes, "The opera ain't over till the fat lady sings."

CHAPTER 9

HOW TO LOVE THIRTY-TWO-HOUR DAYS

I do not know anyone who has got to the top without hard work. That is the recipe. It will not always get you to the top but should get you pretty near.

— MARGARET THATCHER

Without labor, nothing prospers.

— SOPHOCLES

As I said at the outset, I do not intend for this book to be a primer on how to become a hedge fund billionaire. However, I do think it's appropriate to share a few of the insights I've gained along the way about my investment process: what I look for in an employee, my method of management, and my investment philosophy.

I'm a tough boss, as any number of people can tell you. But I am toughest on myself — although I think my former employee Doug

Kass, founder at Seabreeze Partners Management, may have been exaggerating a bit when he told interviewers at CNBC that I was the "James Brown of hedge funds — the hardest working man in the industry." Robert Salomon Jr. — former head of Salomon Brothers Asset Management — was perhaps also a bit over the top when he said of me, "I don't think he puts in long hours. I think he works around the clock. I don't care whether he's on a plane, in a car, or in Florida presumably on vacation — he's working."

In short, I lead by doing. I expect similar effort, performance, and responsiveness from those who work for and with me, and I compensate them accordingly. To justify the high fees that we charged at Omega (generally, 1.5 percent per annum of assets under management and 20 percent on positive performance), we as a team had to bring a total commitment to the business. As at Goldman, anyone who didn't do so simply didn't belong and didn't last long. And this isn't just Goldman and Omega that I'm talking about. This is the culture of our entire industry.

What Makes for a Good Analyst?

A good analyst, like a good sailor, will have a nose for incoming heavy weather and will reef sails accordingly by taking defensive positions. They will also (to mix metaphors from sea to land) not run with the herd as it gallops into the storm.

What other characteristics make for an outstanding analyst/portfolio manager?

1. A desire and commitment to be the best.
2. A strong work ethic.
3. Good communications skills, especially the ability to write a concise summary of their investment opinion.

4. A commitment to penetrating, in-depth research with a strong analytical foundation.

5. An intensity that leads them to always be on top of their positions and ahead of the crowd.

6. A good nose for making money, to know a good idea from a bad one, to make sure the position is meaningful for the organization, to know when to back away when developments are not as anticipated — in sum, to be an effective risk manager.

7. A conviction with respect to investment recommendations and a confidence to add to a position if fundamentals remain intact but the stock is down.

8. An awareness not only of absolute P&L but also of return on capital, and an understanding of the judicious use of capital.

9. Being a team player (particularly important in tapping into the expertise of an organization).

10. Being capable of producing at least three or four core investment ideas, and ten to twelve trading ideas, in a typical year.

11. A pride of ownership, a sense of loyalty to the organization, and a solid commitment to the firm's clients.

12. A personality that is unbiased, skeptical, creative, curious, bold/edgy, and self-aware.

13. An ability to take calculated risks and a willingness to acknowledge and correct mistakes.

14. An ability to identify their comparative advantage and to capitalize on it.

At the most fundamental level, a good analyst should be able to contribute in a manner relevant for a fund. For example, consider a hypothetical $5 billion fund with a team of fifteen investment professionals trying to make 10 to 15 percent (i.e., a $500 million to

$750 million profit). In that case, you want a $35 million to $50 million profit per person. (Bear in mind, it costs the firm more than $1 million just to have the analyst occupy their seat at the table.)

Overall, I've got a pretty good track record concerning people who were with me earlier in their professional lives and then wound up marching on to even greater successes. My former employees include guys who have had terrific careers, including not just Doug Kass but also Larry Robbins (founder of Glenview Capital Management), David Fiszel (founder at Honeycomb Asset Management), Michael Zimmerman (founder of Prentice Capital Management), and Brian Zied (founder of Charter Bridge Capital Management).

It bears repeating: Do what you love and love what you do. Then you won't mind the "thirty-two-hour days." As my friend Warren Buffett puts it, you can "tap dance to work." It's a religion. And it's always been the common denominator between myself and the most successful of those who have worked for me.

Investment Strategy

As for investment strategy, that's something I've alluded to before. I've long practiced the classic value-investing approach, with its focus on picking mispriced (and in my case, mostly undervalued American) stocks selected based on very deep and broad research. We always used an in-depth, microeconomic-analytical approach to inform how much risk to take and when to occasionally dabble in other asset classes such as international stocks, bonds, commodities, equity indexes, and currencies. Although generally long, I would sometimes take short positions against stocks we considered to be overvalued.

What did we look at in any given stock? For starters, of course, the company's price-to-earnings ratio, free cash flow, debt, equity, management, and historical and projected growth, and then such items as, say, the state of labor relations (the "corporate culture") within the firm. Beyond that, one always must look at external events, both real and potential. Is there a trade agreement in the works that, if ratified, might have a negative or positive impact on a given stock or sector? What is the possibility of disruption and/or new competition changing the market landscape for the firm or sector in question? How does the stock compare with other stocks within its sector? As regards, say, a pharmaceutical stock, is there a pending patent expiration that might adversely impact income going forward, or perhaps a new drug in development with a high likelihood of FDA approval that will greatly enhance revenue? It is these types of questions that a good analyst must raise, ponder, and answer before making a buy, sell, or hold recommendation.

Along with microanalysis, it's important to have a realistic sense of the overall market climate. The economy is cyclical. The seed of tomorrow's bull (or bear) market is always in today's bear (or bull) market. John Templeton once brilliantly commented that bull markets are born in pessimism, grow in skepticism, mature in optimism, and die in euphoria. A good analyst develops a sense of where in that cycle we find ourselves at any given moment. I say a *sense* because business cycles are fluid. But telltale signs of a significant market decline are readily identifiable: accelerating/problematic inflation, the prospect of a recession, a hostile Federal Reserve raising interest rates, and — most importantly — investor exuberance.

> The seed of tomorrow's bull (or bear) market is always in today's bear (or bull) market.

Exuberance, also known as *euphoria*. That moment when buying becomes frenetic and price-to-earnings ratios surge to the point of absurdity. That point in time when the general sense of the market is that there's no end in sight for expansion, and there's no such thing as a bubble. That period when averages rise with the same breathless exhilaration as a runaway truck speeding up a steep mountain highway without a headlight, toward an inevitable cliff. That period when you see vast, short-term swings in stock values based on, for the most part, daily headlines rather than sound judgment. That period when the economy and the stock market are both eating their own seed corn, and there's much going on in the way of speculative valuation.

Here I am speaking of such epochs as the excesses of 1972, which led to the bear market of January 1973 to December 1974, and the dot-com bubble of late 1995 through 2000, during which the Nasdaq Composite rose 400 percent only to sink 78 percent from its peak by October 2002. This kind of thing happens and is inevitable, just like hurricanes.

A Few Specifics on Building a Successful Portfolio

At Omega, we attempted to add value to the portfolio in several different, key ways:

- We made forecasts as to the investment environments we anticipated at various periods. In the simplest terms, stocks are high-risk
financial assets, while short-term bonds and cash are low-risk
financial assets. I believe one should only accept stock market
risk when the market is undervalued and likely to rise, and it is
obviously appropriate to avoid risk when the market is overvalued

and likely to fall. This market-direction "call" has always been a very large factor in my determination of risk exposure.

- Most academic studies indicate that asset allocation decisions in any twelve-month period are more important in terms of contribution to portfolio return than specific stock selections. Thus, I've always spent a great deal of time in determining the relative attractiveness of stocks versus bonds in the US and in many non-US markets, and in managing assets accordingly.

- I sometimes take short positions in overvalued securities and markets for both capital gains and hedging purposes.

Basic Analytics

The approach described above is intensely analytical. In pursuing an analysis of the investment environment, I study seven critical "building blocks" encompassing well over one hundred different economic, monetary, and valuation data points. In this process, I analyze the economic environment, monetary policy, valuation data for the aggregate market of over fifteen hundred individual securities, supply/demand patterns within the market as a whole, consumer and investor attitudes and confidence levels, the quantity of attractive investment opportunities (which data contain important information as to a stock market's overall attractiveness), and, lastly, various technical indicators that provide insight into the market's internal structure and health.

While the analysis of so many variables increases the chances of data overload and confused decision-making, I have found over the years that successful investing requires an ability to analyze numerous economic data and valuations, as well as experienced investment judgment, to fully assess the risk characteristics of the investment environment. I want to accept investment risk only when it is compensated for in the market's price structure.

Asset Allocation

After determining our investment outlook, I then concentrate on the asset allocation decision. Arriving at an appropriate asset mix requires a detailed understanding of several factors, some macro in scope and others more portfolio-specific.

The key inputs to the asset mix decision include an overall assessment of the investment outlook and an analysis and valuation of the various financial alternatives available, such as stocks, bonds, and cash. As stated earlier, stocks are high-risk financial assets, and short-duration bonds and cash are low-risk financial assets. I take investment risk when I believe markets are undervalued and likely to rise, and I am defensive when my analysis indicates inadequate returns for risk-taking.

The Stock Selection Process

We at Omega always pursued a rigorous bottom-up approach to stock selection, with particular emphasis on the critical distinction between a company's business value and its market value.

Business value reflects the price an informed buyer would pay for control of a corporation; this is an imprecise concept that can only be estimated with painstaking and exhaustive fundamental analysis. *Market value* reflects the price a marginal investor would pay for a minority position; this is a precise figure that is published daily in the financial press.

Business value, though imprecise, is quite stable and changes only gradually over time; market value, though precise, is extremely volatile and can change dramatically in a single day.

Business value is not affected by market value; market value must eventually reflect business value but often deviates from it by a wide margin.

Business value is determined by a company's economic prospects; market value is determined by the economics of the marketplace (supply and demand).

In estimating a company's business value, I follow an eclectic style that draws on various valuation techniques, since no single method can provide the right answer in all cases. For example, I might focus on asset values (proven reserves) to evaluate an oil company, discounted cash flows (otherwise known as dividends) to evaluate an electric utility, or earnings potential (product pipeline) to evaluate a drug company. Some of the key factors I consider include:

- **Management.** Is management committed to enhancing shareholder value? Is it willing to consider share repurchases when prices fall below fair value? Is it capable of realizing the business potential of an enterprise? What percentage of outstanding shares is held by management?
- **Earnings power and cash flow generation.** What is the company's surplus cash flow position? What are the economics of and prospects for the company's main line of business? What are the company's market position and cost structure? Can the company maintain or expand its profit margins? Are there any unusual investment opportunities available to the company?
- **Asset values.** In what condition are the company's assets, and what would it cost to replace them? Does the company have any hidden assets such as patents, brand names, or franchises that

are not readily apparent in the financial statements? What is the market value of the company's real estate holdings?

- **Risks.** What is the strength of the company's financial position? Can it readily meet its fixed obligations in a bad year? Can it tap the equity and debt markets if needed? How dependent is the company on a single product, customer, or supplier? Are labor relations good and stable? Is the technology stable? Is the company vulnerable to competition from lower-cost imports?

Once business values have been estimated, they must be compared to market prices to arrive at an informed investment decision. I always estimate business value independent of market prices. This keeps my valuation judgments from being swayed by the often-random gyrations of the marketplace. After comparing business value to stock market price, a purchase decision can result from any of three relationships:

- Market price is significantly below business value;
- Market price is at or near business value, but business value is appreciating rapidly; or
- Market price is at or near business value, but asset utilization and business value would improve markedly under different management. Too often, investors purchase stocks based solely on their perceived business values; I believe that comparing business value to market value is essential.

Once the purchase decision has been made, I am not afraid to take a significant and concentrated position in the stock, subject to liquidity, prudence, and diversification. In addition, I closely monitor subsequent market action for opportunities to either increase or lighten my position. In this regard, I strive to maintain a rational, negatively-sloped demand curve where my appetite for a stock will increase when its price goes down and will decrease when its price goes up. Finally, I am equally rigorous concerning my sell discipline, since the sell decision is at least as important to portfolio performance as the purchase decision. I try never to become so enamored of a winning stock that I become married to it, unable to sell after its market price climbs significantly above its business value.

Characteristics of a Good Company

QUALITATIVE

1. Unique — a dominant company selling a useful product or service.
2. Strong, deep management.
3. Innovative.
4. Well controlled.
5. Defined corporate goals.
6. Effective corporate communications.
7. Serving many end-user markets.
8. Price statesmanship in the industry.
9. Limited exposure to import competitions.

QUANTITATIVE

1. Attractively priced.
2. Marketable.
3. Competitive yield and perceived growth prospects for dividends.
4. Less-than-average volatility of earnings and dividends.
5. Above-average unit demand growth.
6. Improving profitability.

7. Well-above-average return on investment.
8. Strong or perceptibly strengthening financial position, with accessibility to debt and equity markets.

The Joy of the Hunt

The joys of microanalysis and portfolio management are, for me, the joys of the hunt. I've gotten paid a lot of money in my career for doing what I genuinely like doing: diving deep into data, seeing something that others don't, making a bet, and having the market prove me right (or wrong).

This, at the end of the day, is the core of my business model and the basis of my success.

PART IV

PHILANTHROPY

CHAPTER 10

NOBLESSE OBLIGE – THE PHILOSOPHY OF PHILANTHROPY

Don't judge each day by the harvest you reap, but by the seeds you plant.

— ROBERT LOUIS STEVENSON

America has a rich tradition of making whipping boys out of those entrepreneurs, investors, and innovators who have done the most, in their times, to move the country forward. The dominant schools of economic and business historians have tended, at least over the past half century or so, to look askance at those who have excelled and, through their successes, greatly increased the wealth and fortunes of the nation and, at the same time, significantly enhanced the standard of living of the average citizen. Somehow, in the folklore of capitalism, an urban legend of rapacious greed and skullduggery has taken root and blossomed regarding many — indeed, a majority — of the country's greatest managerial, speculative, inventive, and commercial talents.

When we think of John D. Rockefeller (1839–1937), for example, the first instinct of many is to imagine a fire-breathing, dollar-clenching monopolist who stomped on the necks of competitors and workers to build a monolithic empire of oil (Standard Oil) over which he alone ruled to the detriment of society, rather than to society's enhancement. This image obscures other truths, such as the humbly-born Rockefeller building a multimillion-dollar enterprise from scratch, his creation of thousands of jobs, and his vast expansion of the country's capacity to refine and distribute oil and oil derivatives, which in turn greatly enabled the expansion of a range of industries throughout the United States.

The image of the evil, money-grubbing capitalist also obscures yet another side of Rockefeller: the Rockefeller who gave half a billion dollars during his lifetime to worthy causes through the Rockefeller Foundation, including the founding of the University of Chicago and of what is today Rockefeller University. As is well known, JDR's generosity has, of course, been continued by his descendants. John Jr. (1874–1960) gave away $537 million during his lifetime, and at his death left $240 million to his numerous descendants. In other words, John Jr. donated 68 percent of his fortune to charity. And Rockefellers are still active philanthropists, acting on a range of fronts.

It is said that Rockefeller Sr. was greatly influenced by the example of charitable giving displayed by the steel magnate Andrew Carnegie (1835–1919). Carnegie is yet another Gilded Age mogul whom the textbooks generally describe as a "Robber Baron," with all the baggage that term implies.

Carnegie, whose father was a poorly paid weaver, had been raised in a one-room cottage in Dunfermline, Scotland, until his family picked up and moved across the Atlantic to Pennsylvania. Although he started with nothing, Carnegie went on to build the Carnegie

Steel Company in Pittsburgh (the forerunner of United States Steel Corporation), which he sold to JPMorgan in 1901. In its time, Carnegie's company played a vital (indeed, indispensable) role in supplying the raw material for the expansion of rail lines and the building of the nation's industrial infrastructure, thus increasing the productivity that made possible the miracle of America's transformation from a stagnant, agrarian society to a rapidly expanding, industrial one.

After the sale of his firm to JPMorgan, Carnegie devoted the remaining eighteen years of his life to philanthropy, eventually giving a total of $350 million dollars (roughly the equivalent of $5.1 billion today) to charity, a sum that equaled more than 95 percent of his total wealth.

In his 1889 essay "Wealth," which was later revised, expanded, and published in a book titled *The Gospel of Wealth*, Carnegie made plain what he believed to be the obligation of the Gilded Age's current generation of self-made men to do good works to the largest degree possible. Furthermore, he insisted that this be done through the building of ladders by which others with ambition might climb to success:

> The problem of our age is the administration of wealth, so that the ties of brotherhood may still bind together the rich and poor in harmonious relationship. The conditions of human life have not only been changed, but revolutionized, within the past few hundred years. In former days there was little difference between the dwelling, dress, food, and environment of the chief and those of his retainers.... The contrast between the palace of the millionaire and the cottage of the laborer with us today measures the change which has come with civilization....

> In bestowing charity, the main consideration should be to help those who will help themselves; to provide part of the means by which those who desire to improve may do so; to give those who desire ... the aids by which they may rise; to assist, but rarely or never to do all....

> In bestowing charity, the main consideration should be to help those who will help themselves; to provide part of the means by which those who desire to improve may do so; to give those who desire ... the aids by which they may rise; to assist, but rarely or never to do all....

Carnegie noted that he'd been inspired in his philanthropy by several prominent men from the previous generation. Among these were Samuel Tilden (1814–1886), who bequeathed $5 million for the creation of the New York Public Library, and Peter Cooper (1791–1883), the son of a hatmaker, who built a fortune through his invention of America's first steam locomotive and then founded New York's Cooper Union for the Advancement of Science and Art.

Carnegie's own giving generally focused on the expansion of the distribution of useful knowledge. Over the course of several decades, he built 2,509 local libraries across the United States. He also established the Carnegie Institution for Science, the Carnegie Trust for the Universities of Scotland, Carnegie Mellon University, the Carnegie Museums of Pittsburgh, and numerous other institutions, including the Carnegie Corporation of New York, which supports educational initiatives nationwide. Among the organizations the latter institution has helped found and fund is the Children's Television Workshop (now called Sesame Workshop), which has helped millions of youngsters get a jump start on their early education through inspired, incisive programming such as the famed *Sesame Street*. In other words, Carnegie's philanthropy, like Rockefeller's and those of the other men named, is ongoing in vital ways even all these years after their deaths. A vibrant legacy.

The list goes on. Another "Robber Baron," Jay Gould (1836–1892), made large but unpublicized gifts to what is today New York University, especially for the enhancement and expansion of the school's Department of Engineering. He was also a major (but anonymous, for he always insisted on anonymity) financial angel supporting the restoration and preservation of George Washington's home, Mount Vernon.

In a later generation, General Motors moguls Charles Stewart Mott (1875–1973) and Alfred P. Sloan (1875–1966) both gave the lion's share of their vast fortunes to charitable endeavors. Over the course of five decades, Mott gave over 90 percent of his total net worth to his Charles Stewart Mott Foundation. Since its founding in 1926, the Mott Foundation has made more than $6 billion in grants and is still involved deeply in good works around the world. Sloan, in turn, gave the bulk of his wealth to establish the Alfred P. Sloan Foundation in 1934, funding research and education in the sciences, technology, economics, and engineering. The Sloan Foundation also funded the establishment of the Alfred P. Sloan School of Management at MIT and the Sloan Kettering Institute and Cancer Center in New York City.

I am pleased to note that my own generation has not been "asleep at the switch" when it comes to philanthropy. I will discuss my personal efforts in the next chapter. But let me now describe the good works of a few of my contemporaries.

My good friend Ken Langone, cofounder of Invemed and Home Depot, is someone I consider something of a brother, as we both had plumbers for fathers. He was raised in a household of modest means on Long Island, and I in a household of modest means in The Bronx.

Ken's education includes an undergraduate degree from Bucknell University and an MBA earned through the night program at the NYU Business School, to which in recent years he's been very generous. This is how Ken tells it in his autobiography *I Love Capitalism!*:

> One day [NYU Business School Dean George Daly] came to see me at Invemed, and I told him how grateful I was for the night program but said I was worried about the school's future. NYU Law School, I reminded him, used to have a night program that they ended because they felt it detracted from the school's stature. I worried aloud that a similar mind-set might lead to the end of the business school's night program.
>
> Daly told me that wasn't going to happen. "We're known for our part-time program," he said.
>
> Then he asked me if I'd be willing to make a major gift to help it along.
>
> At that point, Home Depot was on its feet and expanding aggressively; Invemed was doing well. I was just starting to feel pretty flush. And so I said yes to George Daly. I made the business school a gift of $10 million, and they renamed the night program the Langone MBA for Working Professionals. By the way, naming it after me was the school's idea. Not mine.

Ken has also given $100 million to NYU Langone Medical Center and has made many other substantial gifts to a range of major institutions over the past several decades, including the Boys' Club of New York, Bucknell University, and the Harlem Children's Zone — especially its Promise Academy, a charter school fully funded by Ken. As a devout Roman Catholic (knighted by the Pope into the Pontifical Equestrian Order of St. Gregory the Great), Ken has also been a significant benefactor helping with the restoration of New York's St. Patrick's Cathedral:

> The Bible says there's a better chance of a camel getting through the eye of a needle than a rich man making it to heaven. The Bible says that if I want to be *really* rich, I'll give everything away. Warren Buffett's a little less strict than Scripture: he says that wealthy people should give away at least half their wealth to philanthropic causes. I signed Warren's Giving Pledge years ago, but in my case it was academic: I'd already given away more than half my net worth....

> Too many people measure success the wrong way. Money should be at the bottom of the list, not the top. I woke up soon enough to realize that if the only way you can define my life is by the size of my bank account, then I've failed. Fifteen or twenty years ago, a guy asked me how much I was worth, and I answered without thinking, "My net worth is what good I do with what I have."

My old Columbia Business School chum Mario Gabelli has also become an active philanthropist. Mario, another signatory to Buffett's

Giving Pledge, has in recent years given $15 million to Columbia Business School, more than $60 million to Fordham University (his undergraduate alma mater), and numerous other significant gifts to organizations and institutions ranging from Boston College to the Ellis Island Foundation and Miami University, as well as to New York City Local 6 and the Hotel and Gaming Trades Council, the latter in memory of his father, a line cook at Lüchow's who was a member of that union.

Warren Buffett has said, "If you're in the luckiest 1 percent of humanity, you owe it to the rest of humanity to think about the other 99 percent." Charles Dickens, who spent almost as much time on philanthropic endeavors as he did on his writing, commented, "No one is useless in this world who lightens the burdens of another." John F. Kennedy made a related point: "Philanthropy, charity, giving voluntarily and freely — call it what you like, but it is truly a jewel in the American tradition."

It truly is a jewel in the American tradition, and one that shines just as brightly today as it has in the past. Just consider the Bill & Melinda Gates Foundation, with an endowment of more than $45 billion dollars (including many billions entrusted to them by Buffett) and its support of myriad programs for the betterment of mankind, from curing disease to mastering the climate crisis.

It all boils down to the idea of *noblesse oblige* — nobility obliges. To whom much is given, much is expected.

Or, as Ralph Waldo Emerson put it: "Superior advantages bind you to larger generosity."

So far as I am concerned, it should be no other way.

CHAPTER 11

MY PHILANTHROPIC WORK THUS FAR

We make a living by what we get. We make a life by what we give.

— WINSTON CHURCHILL

For some reason, Senator Elizabeth Warren (D-Massachusetts) has made a fetish of not only criticizing me but also mocking me in public. I'm not sure what it is about me in particular, among so many other wealthy people, that fascinates her so. There are plenty of other hardworking, successful folks whom she could target in her long-standing war against capitalism. But in choosing me, she has made something of a strategic mistake, as I'm in the process of giving away every cent of what she no doubt believes are my ill-gotten gains.

Elizabeth Warren is a politician in the worst sense of the word. She is not a stupid woman, but she consciously says stupid things and makes absurd proposals that she knows will never fly, because she likes to play into all-too-easy and simplistic themes of class warfare. (Why so many people want to "eat the rich" is beyond me. I doubt if we'd taste all that great.)

In one of her many pithy Tweets, Warren accurately described me as someone who has benefited greatly from the opportunities afforded me in this country but then demanded that I "pitch in" to help others find their American dream. This was her response to my well-founded criticism of her dumb idea for a "wealth tax." By responding in this manner — attacking me personally rather than defending her point of view — she revealed much about her personality and demonstrated that she knows about as much about me as she does about economics. I wonder how much of her wealth Elizabeth Warren has given away, as I'm giving away 100 percent of mine. How is that for pitching in?

After her attack on me — not just via Tweet but on television, in print media, and elsewhere during her disastrous 2019–2020 campaign for the Democratic presidential nomination — I wrote Warren a five-page open letter to which (you'll spot a trend here) I received no response:

October 30, 2019

Senator Elizabeth A. Warren
309 Hart Senate Office Building
Washington, DC 20510

Dear Senator Warren:

While I am not a Twitter user, several friends passed along to me your October 23rd tweet in which, after correctly observing that my financial success can be attributed, in no small measure, to the many opportunities which this great country has afforded me, you proceeded to admonish me (as if a parent chiding an ungrateful child) to "pitch in a bit more so everyone else has a chance at the American dream, too." Our political differences aside, your tweet demonstrated a fundamental misunderstanding of who I am, what I stand for, and why I believe so many of your economic policy initiatives are misguided. Because your tweet was publicly disseminated, I feel compelled to respond in the form of an Open Letter for all who are interested to read.

As I have noted elsewhere, mine is a classic American success story. I have been richly rewarded by a life of hard work combined with a great deal of good luck, including that to have been born in a country that adheres to an ethos of upward mobility for determined strivers. My father was a plumber who practiced his trade in the South Bronx after he and my mother emigrated from Poland. I was the first member of my family to earn a college degree. I benefitted from both a good public education system (all the way through college) and my parents' constant prodding. When I joined Goldman Sachs following graduation from Columbia Business School, I had no money in the bank, a negative net worth, a National Defense Education Act student loan to repay, and a six-month-old baby (not to mention his mother, my wife of now 55 years) to support. I had a successful, near-25-year run at Goldman before leaving to start a private investment firm. As a result of my good fortune, I have been able to donate in philanthropy many times more than I have spent on myself over a lifetime, and I am not finished; I have subscribed to the Buffett/Gates Giving Pledge to ensure that my money, properly stewarded, continues to do some good after I'm gone. As I told Mr. Buffett when I joined the Pledge, asking for half of my money wasn't enough; I intend to donate substantially all of it. Apart from my children and grandchildren, I cannot imagine a finer legacy.

My story is far from unique. I know many people who are similarly situated, by both humble origin and hard-won accomplishment, whose greatest joy in life is to use their resources to improve their communities. Many of their names — including those of Ken Langone, Carl Icahn and Sandy Weill, all self-made billionaires whom I am proud to call friends — are associated with major hospitals (NYU Langone Health, Icahn School of Medicine at Mount Sinai, Weill Cornell Medical College, and, in my own case, Saint Barnabas Medical Center and Boca Raton Regional Hospital) which tend to the needs of, among others, many thousands of poor patients each year who could not otherwise afford the best-of-class medical services that those fine institutions, with our support and that of others like us, provide.

Having grown up without much money and valuing highly the public education I received, I have donated substantial sums to Hunter College of the City University of New York and to Columbia University's

Graduate School of Business — money for scholarships, libraries, and the construction of new buildings. In 2014, with a very large gift, I established Cooperman College Scholars, a program which identifies academically talented, highly motivated students of strong character in Essex County (including Newark), New Jersey, who are traditionally underrepresented in higher education — children of color, impoverished children, children facing situational challenges that tug them away from educational priorities — and, through a combination of high-school counseling, tuition grants, and ongoing cohort-based mentoring to help matriculated students navigate the challenges of transitioning successfully to college life — and by eliminating the negative impact of insufficient financial aid and social support systems on student persistence and graduation rates — enables them to attend college, thrive there and graduate. It is our goal to put 500 district and charter public-school students through college in the next few years. As I stated when my gift was announced, for splendid youngsters such as these to be denied access to a higher education, and to all the opportunities that that can afford, simply because of financial need is a national tragedy. My family feels very privileged to be in a position where we can help at least some of these children's dreams come true, and in the process fundamentally change their lives.

However much it resonates with your base, your vilification of the rich is misguided, ignoring, among other things, the sources of their wealth and the substantial contributions to society which they already, unprompted by you, make. Typically, unless born to money or married into it, people become rich by providing a product or service that others want and are willing to pay for.

- Ken Langone, Bernie Marcus and Arthur Blank founded Home Depot in 1978 with $2 million raised from 40 friends — none of whom were wealthy by your standards (average investment $50,000) — after Bernie (age 49) and Arthur (age 36) had been fired from their previous jobs and — with three children each, no health insurance, no savings, and heavily mortgaged homes — were effectively broke. The rest is history. From nothing, Home Depot has grown into an enterprise with a market capitalization of over $250 billion that provides employment to more than four-hundred thousand workers — thousands of whom became millionaires investing in the company's stock — while the founders have given away in excess of $1 billion in charitable donations (and still counting).

- In 1981, Mike Bloomberg, whose record of public service and philanthropy are legendary, created a machine that changed the way the financial world — a sector that is the source of much of the tax revenues that fuel your legislative priorities — conducts business. Today, Bloomberg L.P. has morphed into a diversified financial-services company that employs 20,000 people.

- In 1998, computer scientists Larry Page and Sergey Brin, while still in graduate school, founded Google, now one of the foremost search engines that power the Internet. Today, Google employs more than 100,000 workers, and Page and Brin have donated billions of dollars each to charitable causes.

The list goes on and on of self-made billionaires — Bill Gates (Microsoft Corporation — 144,000 jobs), Michael Dell (Dell Technologies — 145,000 jobs), Mark Zuckerberg (Facebook — 39,000 jobs) and Larry Ellison (Oracle Corporation — 137,000 jobs), among others — who have built huge businesses from the ground up, providing jobs and economic opportunity to hundreds of thousands of taxpaying workers, and voluntarily gift every year, in the aggregate, billions of dollars back to the society that nurtured their success. Their stories, and many more like them, are the very embodiment of the American Dream. For you to suggest that capitalism is a dirty word and that these people, as a group, are ingrates who didn't earn their riches, through strenuous effort and (in many cases) paradigm-shifting insights, and now don't pull their weight societally indicates that you either are grossly uninformed or are knowingly warping the facts for narrow political gain.

Now for your soak-the-rich positions on taxes and economic policy.

The two University of California at Berkeley economists who are advising your campaign, Emmanuel Saez and Gabriel Zucman, have drawn a lot of media attention for their contention that the U.S. federal income tax system is flat, which is to say, regressive and therefore fundamentally unfair to low-income Americans. But their analysis is open to challenge, and the conclusions which they (and you) draw from it are debatable.

- As others have pointed out, Saez and Zucman focus on gross, not net, taxes, ignoring transfer payments (Social Security, Medicare and Medicaid benefits) which are disproportionately paid to the poor and middle class, and whose inclusion in their tax-burden calculations would materially skew the outcome in the opposite direction.
- They include excise and sales taxes which are by their nature regressive (and therefore overstate the outsized tax burden on low-income Americans) but have nothing to do with federal fiscal policy and tax-code structure — it's simply how state and local governments have chosen to fund themselves; excluding those and similar taxes from their analysis would again yield a result counter to the economists' thesis.

- By focusing on current-year rather than lifetime tax burdens, Saez and Zucman understate taxes on the rich (who are taxed both on current year's income and on future dividends, interest and capital gains earned on savings) and overstate those on the poor and middle class (since future transfer-payment benefits, which as noted are excluded from the economists' calculations, comprise an increasing share of their financial resources as they age).

In sum, Saez and Zucman's economic model appears to be based on highly dubious assumptions and tailored to promote a specific "progressive" policy agenda, and their conclusions are far less definitive and unequivocal than they maintain.

Further undercutting your economists' fair-share arguments, the Internal Revenue Service recently released data that detail, for tax year 2016 (the latest year for which these data are available), individual federal income tax shares according to income percentile.

- As a percentage of total individual federal income taxes paid, the top 1% of taxpayers paid a greater share of that total (37.3%) than the bottom 90% combined (30.5%).
- As a percentage of taxpayers' adjusted gross income paid in individual federal income taxes, the top 1% of taxpayers paid an effective tax

rate (26.9%) which was more than seven times higher than that of the bottom 50% (3.7%).

- The top 50% of taxpayers paid 97% of all individual federal income taxes; the bottom 50% paid the remaining 3%.

As analyzed by the Tax Foundation, a leading independent tax-policy nonprofit, the data demonstrate "that the U.S. individual income tax continues to be very progressive, borne primarily by the highest income earners."

Saez and Zucman surface again in the debate over an explicit, recurring wealth tax (as distinct from property and one-time estate taxes — alternative forms of levy on wealth) targeting the richest Americans, a major plank of your economic platform. As numerous economists (if not yours) have observed, the history and prognosis of explicit wealth taxes is not sanguine.

- In a February 2018 article for the International Monetary Fund, the authors, economists James Brumby and Michael Keen, noted that "there are now very few effective explicit wealth taxes in either developing or advanced economies. Indeed between 1985 and 2007, the number of OECD countries with an active wealth tax fell from twelve to just four. And many of those were, and are, of limited effectiveness."
- At a recent conference sponsored by the Peterson Institute for International Economics,

Saez and Zucman debated their advocacy of a wealth tax with Harvard economists Lawrence Summers (Bill Clinton's Treasury Secretary and Barack Obama's Director of the National Economic Council) and Gregory Mankiw (George W. Bush's Chair of the Council of Economic Advisers). Your economists made the case that federal tax revenues should be raised to finance increased expenditures on education, infrastructure and healthcare subsidization, but as Mankiw and Summers argued, whether an explicit wealth tax is the preferred route is at best questionable — plagued by issues of constitutionality, tax avoidance, asset valuation and administrability — and the assumptions underlying Saez and Zucman's analysis are, as noted, suspect. As Summers put it: "For progressives to use their energy on a proposal that has a more than 50% chance of being struck down by the Supreme Court, little chance of passing through Congress, and whose revenue-raising potential is very much in doubt, is to potentially sacrifice immense opportunities."

The opportunities to which Summers was referring — opportunities to raise funds for a more progressive legislative agenda that might stand a chance of passing Congress and weathering constitutional scrutiny, and whose revenue-raising potential is unquestionable — could include eliminating the exemption of capital gains from taxation upon death, the carried-interest exemption for private equity and hedge funds, and the capital-gains tax-deferral preference accorded like-kind exchanges under Section 1031 of the Internal Revenue Code.

It may be worth considering that wealth redistribution advocates might be wrong to focus solely on income *inequality* rather than on income *opportunity* more broadly. In economics, the most commonly used gauge of economic inequality across a target population is the Gini coefficient (or Gini index), named for the Italian statistician who developed it in 1912. A Gini coefficient of zero means the country has perfect equality of financial prosperity; a coefficient of one means maximum inequality. The World Bank, in its Gini coefficient-by-country analysis for 2019, ranks a number of countries — including Afghanistan, Albania, Algeria, Kyrgyzstan, Moldova, Romania, Slovakia, Slovenia and Ukraine, all with Gini coefficients in the 20s — high on its financial equality list. Yet despite the relatively high degree of financial equality implied by their numbers, none of these countries can boast booming economies or generalized income and wealth-creation opportunities. It would therefore appear that their citizens may be more aligned than those of most other countries in the fair distribution of wealth, but that does not translate in any meaningful sense into widespread prosperity. So what good is income equality to them? Should that — the narrowing of income inequality as an end in itself, as opposed to income growth for all — really be our fiscal policy imperative?

And that takes me to my final points — what I do, in fact, believe should be our fiscal policy priorities:

- Rather than adopt an explicit wealth tax whose efficacy has been widely debunked by experience around the world, let's debate what the maximum individual and corporate tax rates should be. I believe in a progressive income tax structure. The wealthy *should* pay more than those of lesser means, but they already do, and at some point, higher effective (federal, state and local combined) rates become confiscatory. That should never be the ethos of this country. I am on record as having said that I don't mind working six months of the year for the government and six months for myself, paying an effective combined tax rate of 50% on my income. But many who live in high-tax cities and states pay even more, while some of the nation's highest earners pay less. A more effective way than a wealth tax to right-size the latter imbalance might be to revisit some form of the Buffett Rule (repeatedly rejected by Congress since it was first proposed in 2012), which would implement a surtax on taxpayers making over a million dollars a year to better ensure that the highest earners pay their fair share.

- Let's eliminate loopholes in our tax code that allow so much seepage through the cracks. A good start would be the short-list enumerated several paragraphs above.

- Before levying more taxes of any stripe, candidates should commit to trying to fund their agendas through revenue-neutral proposals that would cull bureaucratic waste. I have seen too much evidence of governmental profligacy to have much faith in Congress's ability to spend our tax revenues efficiently. Frustrated efforts to privatize the U.S. Postal Service, which loses billions of dollars a year as a government-owned corporation, are a case in point. Social progress does not have to come at the cost of further administrative bloat.

I am a registered Independent who votes the issues and the person, not the party. The fact is, Senator Warren, that despite our philosophical differences, we should be working together to find common ground in this vital conversation — not firing off snarky tweets that stir your base at the expense of accuracy. Let's elevate the dialogue and find ways to keep this a land of opportunity where hard work, talent and luck are rewarded and everyone gets a fair shot at realizing the American Dream.

Sincerely,

Leon G. Cooperman

Yes, the American free market has treated me very well, although I feel that I have worked very hard for every dime I've earned.

That being said, there are only so many things one can do with wealth.

The first is self-indulgence. Some people collect art. Others collect sports teams, cars, yachts, and mansions. Perhaps I'm a hick, but I'm not particularly interested in art, sports teams, or yachting. I drive a Hyundai, even though at my principal home in Florida I'm surrounded by people driving Bentleys and Rolls-Royces. My two homes, in Florida and New Jersey (the latter being where my wife and I have lived for decades and raised our family), are quite comfortable but by no means mansions. Possessions, to my mind, are by and large annoyances. More to keep track of and administer. I'm a "less is more" kind of guy.

The second way you can use your wealth is to leave it to your children and grandchildren. I've got two sons who have done very well for themselves — one a money manager and the other a scientist — and don't need any financial aid from me. I also have grandchildren whom I love dearly, but to pass significant wealth on to your offspring is, I think, a bad idea, as it disallows them their own self-achievement and success.

The third approach is to give your wealth to the government. No way. Only a schnook would give the government more than he is required to by law. P. J. O'Rourke once commented that giving government money and power is like giving teenage boys liquor and car keys, and I heartily agree. My money can be put to far better use elsewhere.

Speaking of which, the final and best use for wealth is philanthropy.

It was back in September 2010 that Toby and I sat down to dinner with Warren Buffett, Michael Bloomberg (then mayor of New

York City), and Bill and Melinda Gates to discuss Warren's Giving Pledge, to which I subsequently subscribed. I mentioned to Warren in a note following our dinner:

> Toby and I very much enjoyed our dinner with you, Bill, Melinda and Mayor Mike. The graciousness of the mayor's hospitality was matched only by the interesting guests and the quality of the dinner conversation! The concept of the Giving Pledge is intriguing and meritorious. The fact that Toby and I are even candidates to make the pledge is a testimony to the American Dream. Let me explain.
>
> I am the son of a plumber who practiced his trade in the South Bronx. I am the first generation American born in my family as well as the first to get a college degree. My education is largely public school based — public grade school, high school and college all in The Bronx. I had a short stint at the Columbia University Graduate School of Business where I earned an MBA and this opened the door for me to Goldman Sachs. I joined the Firm the day after graduation as I had a National Defense Education Act Student Loan to repay, had no money in the bank, and a six-month-old child to support. I had a near 25-year run of happiness and good fortune at Goldman Sachs. The last 19 years at Omega have also been years of happiness and good fortune with a few bumps along the way. While I worked hard, I must say I had more than my share of good luck.

Toby and I feel it is our moral imperative to give others the opportunity to pursue the American Dream by sharing our financial success.... [It is] written in the Talmud that "A man's net worth is measured not by what he earns but rather what he gives away." It is in this spirit that we enthusiastically agree to take the Giving Pledge.

I've already mentioned Toby's and my substantial gifts to such institutions as the City University of New York, Columbia University, our Cooperman College Scholars Program, and other worthy institutions and causes. Still, there are a few more highlights that I'd like to point out.

In general, with a few exceptions, there have been two themes to our giving: education and healthcare. Overall, the nature of our giving was best summarized by a 2021 article in *New Jersey Jewish News*:

Cooperman's philanthropic donations are nearing the billion-dollar mark and tally up as impressive and eclectic, with an emphasis on paying it forward. "There's no shortage of worthwhile organizations.... As you get more visibility, more people come to you and you've got to discern." The Coopermans are reluctant to talk about specific figures out of an abundance of modesty, but research and records tell the story.

One of the most visible signs of their generosity is evident to patients, staff, and visitors at Saint Barnabas Medical Center in Livingston, where the gleaming Cooperman Family Pavilion opened a few years ago after a gift of $25 million, this followed by another $100 million. The Coopermans also donated an equal amount to the Boca Raton Regional Hospital in Florida. And the family will have its name added to the soon-to-debut [headquarters] of the [organization] Jewish Services for the Developmentally Disabled, also in Livingston, after a $2 million gift. Birthright Israel benefited from a $20 million bequest, while the state's premier arts venue, New Jersey PAC in Newark, received $20 million. JCC MetroWest and Daughters of Israel, both in West Orange, were recipients of more than $6 million and $1 million respectively.

Being a hands-on guy, Mr. Cooperman also supported Meals on Wheels in his old Bronx neighborhood with both donations and deliveries. He and his wife continue to be enthusiastic supporters of the ECLC [Education, Careers and Lifelong Community] in Chatham, where Toby Cooperman spent 35 years working with disabled, neurologically impaired children. And lesser-known charities come into play too, such as the Songs of Love Foundation, which uses volunteers to customize lyrics and music for hospital-ized kids with severe or terminal illnesses …

I should point out that once Toby and I are gone, whatever remains of our wealth will reside in a charitable foundation to be administered by our children and grandchildren as they see fit.

Toby and I consider ourselves blessed to be able to do such things as double the size of hospitals and put hundreds of deserving under-privileged kids through college. But of course, not everyone is so blessed (or lucky) as we are. Nevertheless, everyone can give *something* back, as their resources permit. Small donations are as important as large ones, and in volume they are often more important than large ones. As well, in some cases, simple *time* — volunteering — is the greatest gift possible.

> Everyone can give *something* back, as their resources permit.

Theodore Roosevelt once said, "Do what you can, with what you have, where you are."

In the final analysis, it's as simple as that.

PART V

POLITICAL PHILOSOPHY

CHAPTER 12

CAPITALISM WORKS

What our generation has forgotten is that the system of private property is the most important guarantee of freedom, not only for those who own property, but scarcely less for those who do not. It is only because the control of the means of production is divided among many people acting independently that nobody has complete power over us, that we as individuals can decide what to do with ourselves.

— ECONOMIST FRIEDRICH AUGUST HAYEK,

1944, THE ROAD TO SERFDOM

I became concerned recently when I saw an Axios poll indicating that among young Americans (eighteen to twenty-four), regardless of political persuasion, capitalism had only a 42 percent positive rating, while the negative view garnered 54 percent. I have a feeling that much of this thinking is the result of a general ignorance about command economies and their myriad inefficiencies and also a general misunderstanding of what free markets are (and are not). My hunch is that the statistics relate to a general impression among the young that the economy is somehow rigged — that the capitalist model represents some sort of zero-sum game, where one person *has* only because another person *hasn't*. Of course, that's entirely not the case; indeed, nothing could be further from the truth.

Much of the skepticism about the capitalist model has been stoked by the class-warfare rhetoric of such politicos as Sen. Elizabeth Warren (D-MA), Rep. Alexandria Ocasio-Cortez (AOC; D-NY), and former Pres. Barack Obama. Regarding the latter, I was moved to write an open letter in November 2011.

President Barack Obama
The White House
1600 Pennsylvania Avenue NW
Washington, D.C. 20500

November 28, 2011

Dear Mr. President,

It is with a great sense of disappointment that I write this. Like many others, I hoped that your election would bring a salutary change of direction to the country, despite what more than a few feared was an overly aggressive social agenda. And I cannot credibly blame you for the economic mess that you inherited, even if the policy response on your watch has been profligate and largely ineffectual. (You did not, after all, invent TARP.) I understand that when surrounded by cries of "the end of the world as we know it is nigh," even the strongest of minds may have a tendency to shoot first and aim later in a well-intended effort to stave off the predicted apocalypse.

But what I can justifiably hold you accountable for is your and your minions' role in setting the tenor of the rancorous debate now roiling us that smacks of what so many have characterized as "class warfare." Whether this reflects your principled belief that the eternal divide between the haves and have-nots is at the root of all the evils that afflict our society or just a cynical, populist appeal to his base by a president struggling in the polls is of little importance. What does matter is that the divisive, polarizing tone of your rhetoric is cleaving a widening gulf, at this point as much visceral as philosophical, between the down-trodden and those best positioned to help them. It is a gulf that is at once counterproductive and freighted with dangerous historical precedents. And it is an approach to governing that owes more to desperate demagoguery than your Administration should feel comfortable with.

Just to be clear, while I have been richly rewarded by a life of hard work (and a great deal of luck), I was not to-the-manor-born. My father was a plumber who practiced his trade in the South Bronx after he and my mother emigrated from Poland. I was the first member of my family to earn a college degree. I benefited from both a good public education system (P.S. 75, Morris High School and Hunter College, all in The Bronx) and my parents' constant prodding. When I joined Goldman Sachs following graduation from Columbia University's business school, I had no money in the bank, a negative net worth, a National

Defense Education Act student loan to repay, and a six-month-old child (not to mention his mother, my wife of now 47 years) to support. I had a successful, near-25-year run at Goldman, which I left 20 years ago to start a private investment firm. As a result of my good fortune, I have been able to give away to those less blessed far more than I have spent on myself and my family over a lifetime, and last year I subscribed to Warren Buffett's Giving Pledge to ensure that my money, properly stewarded, continues to do some good after I'm gone.

My story is anything but unique. I know many people who are similarly situated, by both humble family history and hard-won accomplishment, whose greatest joy in life is to use their resources to sustain their communities. Some have achieved a level of wealth where philanthropy is no longer a by-product of their work but its primary impetus. This is as it should be. We feel privileged to be in a position to give back, and we do. My parents would have expected nothing less of me.

I am not, by training or disposition, a policy wonk, polemicist or pamphleteer. I confess admiration for those who, with greater clarity of expression and command of the relevant statistical details, make these same points with more eloquence and authoritativeness than I can hope to muster. For recent examples, I would point you to "Hunting the Rich" (Leaders, *The Economist*, September 24, 2011), "The Divider vs.

the Thinker" (Peggy Noonan, *The Wall Street Journal*, October 29, 2011), "Wall Street Occupiers Misdirect Anger" (Christine Todd Whitman, *Bloomberg*, October 31, 2011), and "Beyond Occupy" (Bill Keller, *The New York Times*, October 31, 2011) — all, if you haven't read them, making estimable work of the subject.

But as a taxpaying businessman with a weekly payroll to meet and more than a passing familiarity with the ways of both Wall Street and Washington, I do feel justified in asking you: Is the tone of the current debate really constructive?

People of differing political persuasions can (and do) reasonably argue about whether, and how high, tax rates should be hiked for upper-income earners; whether the Bush-era tax cuts should be extended or permitted to expire, and for whom; whether various deductions and exclusions under the federal tax code that benefit principally the wealthy and multinational corporations should be curtailed or eliminated; whether unemployment benefits and the payroll tax cut should be extended; whether the burdens of paying for the nation's bloated entitlement programs are being fairly spread around, and whether those programs themselves should be reconfigured in light of current and projected budgetary constraints; whether financial institutions deemed "too big to fail" should be serially bailed out or broken up first, like an earlier era's trusts, because they pose a systemic risk and their size benefits no one but their owners; whether the solution to what ails us as a nation is an amalgam of more regulation, wealth redistribution, and a greater concentration of power in a central government that has proven no more (I'm being charitable here) adept than the private sector in reining in the excesses that brought us to this pass — the list goes on and on, and the dialectic is admirably American. Even though, as a high-income taxpayer, I might be considered one of its targets, I find this reassessment of so many entrenched economic premises healthy and long overdue. Anyone who could survey today's challenging fiscal landscape, with an un- and under-employment rate of nearly 20 percent and roughly 40 percent of the country on public assistance, and not acknowledge an imperative for change is either heartless, brainless, or running for office on a very parochial agenda. And if I end up paying more taxes as a result, so be it. The alternatives are all worse.

But what I do find objectionable is the highly politicized idiom in which this debate is being conducted. Now, I am not naïve. I understand that in today's America, this is how the business of governing typically gets done — a situation that, given the gravity of our problems, is as deplorable as it is seemingly ineluctable. But as President first and foremost and leader of your party second, you should endeavor to rise above the partisan fray and raise the level of discourse to one that is both more civil and more conciliatory, that seeks collaboration over confrontation. That is what "leading by example" means to most people.

Capitalism is not the source of our problems, as an economy or as a society, and capitalists are not the scourge that they are too often made out to be. As a group, we employ many millions of taxpaying people, pay their salaries, provide them with health-care coverage, start new companies, found new industries, create new products, fill store shelves at Christmas, and keep the wheels of commerce and progress (and indeed of government, by generating the income whose taxation funds it) moving. To frame the debate as one of rich-and-entitled versus poor-and-dispossessed is to both miss the point and further inflame an already incendiary environment. It is also a naked, political pander to some of the basest human emotions — a strategy, as history teaches, that never ends well for anyone but totalitarians and anarchists.

With due respect, Mr. President, it's time for you to throttle-down the partisan rhetoric and appeal to people's better instincts, not their worst. Rather than assume that the wealthy are a monolithic, selfish and unfeeling lot who must be subjugated by the force of the state, set a tone that encourages people of good will to meet in the middle. When you were a community organizer in Chicago, you learned the art of waging a guerilla campaign against a far superior force. But you've graduated from that milieu and now help to set the agenda for that superior force. You might do well at this point to eschew the polarizing vernacular of political militancy and become the transcendent leader you were elected to be. You are likely to be far more effective, and history is likely to treat you far more kindly, for it.

Sincerely yours,

Leon G. Cooperman

It is only within a capitalist system that a man or woman can start with next to nothing and, through ability, effort, and good fortune, rise to wealth and prominence. That has been the case with Ken Langone, Mario Gabelli, and countless others, including me.

In 2015, I was honored to receive the Horatio Alger Award from the Horatio Alger Association of Distinguished Americans. This Association was established in 1947 and references the many "rags to riches" stories written by Alger (1832–1899), all of them meant to encourage American youth to aspire to great things, no matter how humble their origins. In 2022, I sponsored my friend Mario Gabelli for the same honor, which he received along with actress Jane Seymour, football running back Herschel Walker, and thirteen others, all of whom came from quite modest backgrounds to achieve excellence and success in their chosen fields. (Ken Langone received the award in 2012 and Charles Stewart Mott in 1971.) Through 2022, there have been more than 770 such honorees, a testament to the financial and social mobility possible in our system. These honorees have included Hank

> We continue to fuel the engine that enables the rise of those willing to work for success in this, the best of all possible economic systems.

Aaron, Buzz Aldrin, Maya Angelou, Bob Hope, Waylon Jennings, Pearl Buck, Denzel Washington, and Quincy Jones, to mention just a few notables.

But the Horatio Alger Association is much more than just some sort of self-congratulatory glee club. In fact, the main purpose of the organization is to provide support services and scholarships to deserving undergraduates from low-income families, and it has been doing so for a very long time. In 2022, some eighteen hundred students received Alger scholarships totaling $18 million. Through 2023, the Association expects to have given away some $245 million to thirty-five thousand students overall. In this way, members of the Association — most of whom have already "given back" in numerous ways — give back even a bit more.

We are, of course, happy to be able to do so.

And in that way, we continue to fuel the engine that enables the rise of those willing to work for success in this, the best of all possible economic systems.

Capitalism works!

CHAPTER 13

OF LIGADO AND INHOFE

My faith in the people governing is, on the whole, infinitesimal;
my faith in the people governed is, on the whole, illimitable.

— CHARLES DICKENS

In 1972, David Halberstam published a book about how the Kennedy/Johnson cabinets got us, senselessly, into the deadly and pointless quagmire of the Vietnam War. They'd screwed up royally, and Halberstam's title, *The Best and the Brightest*, was meant to be a blisteringly ironic rebuke. Many years later, the writer and political satirist P. J. O'Rourke quipped, "The best and the brightest do not go into politics. The best and the brightest are at Goldman Sachs." In general, I feel O'Rourke was correct. This is not to say the best and the brightest go *only* to Wall Street, but in my experience, they *do* tend to go into the private sector — a place where quality counts, competition drives productivity, deadlines and benchmarks are serious, and the ultimate proof of anything is solid results.

Things tend to be quantifiable in the private sector: either the office tower gets built or it doesn't; either the books balance or they don't; either sales goals and benchmarks are met or they aren't. There is little room for rhetoric, artifice, or posturing in the private sector. The profit motive brings with it clarity, discipline, and (in general) order.

There is an old *Peanuts* cartoon that shows Charlie Brown and Lucy lying flat on the grass, gazing up at the sky. Lucy asks, "Do all fairytales start with 'Once upon a time' Charlie Brown?" To this, Charlie responds, "No, a lot of them start with 'If elected, I promise to ...'"

> There is little room for rhetoric, artifice, or posturing in the private sector. The profit motive brings with it clarity, discipline, and (in general) order.

The most effective of our elected officials have tended to be businessmen first and foremost who later entered politics as an act of public service. Michael Bloomberg is a shining example of this: a self-made business success who built a stellar technology and news organization from nothing, became a billionaire, and then went into politics to become a three-term mayor of New York City and put the city back on its feet after years of poor administration. Another example is the General Motors mogul Charles Stewart Mott who, after making his fortune, served several terms as the mayor of Flint, Michigan, in the early part of the twentieth century, bringing with him business efficiency and balanced budgets and greatly advancing the growth of that town's infrastructure and industry. I hasten to add, however, that I would not include former President Donald Trump with such men as these, as to my mind he has been a failure in everything, both business and the presidency. I hold no brief for Donald Trump.

At one point, back in 2011, during the Obama administration, I briefly considered a presidential bid. I even went so far as to map out a nine-point platform:

1. Get out of Iraq and Afghanistan. Provide every returning soldier with a free four-year college education or training at a trade school of their choice.

2. Set up a peacetime Works Progress Administration effort to channel a portion of the savings into rebuilding US infrastructure.

3. Unleash the domestic energy industry to develop domestic energy supplies and reserves. This will create employment and reduce our dependency on foreign suppliers.

4. Government spending should be limited to a growth rate at least 1 percent below the level of nominal gross domestic product growth.

5. Freeze entitlements and raise the Social Security retirement age to seventy with an exception for those that work at hard labor.

6. Ten percent income tax surcharge for three years on those who earn over $500,000 per year.

7. Five percent value-added tax to get at the underground economy and deal with the deficit.

8. Tackle healthcare in a serious way.

9. Reinstate the "uptick" rule for short sales, ban or curtail high-frequency trading, and limit credit default swap trading to those who own the underlying bonds. The high-frequency traders are turning the best capital market in the world into a casino and scaring the public. This is not in the public interest.

Late that summer, in a somewhat tongue-in-cheek manner, I mentioned my interest in the presidency to my Omega investors during a conference call and revealed my nine-point platform. As I subsequently told Warren Buffett, "Much to my surprise, I had near unanimous support for my possible candidacy, though I suspect it was more related to getting me out of Omega than getting me into the White House!" In turn, I sent Warren my nine points and asked him point-blank what he thought should be the maximum tax rate on ordinary income for the highest earners in the country. His response was the following:

> Dear Lee:
>
> If you run for president, I can deliver Nebraska. Just let me know when to gear up.
>
> There are two possible approaches to increasing the rates on those having taxable $1 million or more with a second step-up at $10 million. One would be to increase the rate at $1 million by five points and at $10 million at ten points.
>
> Another approach would certainly be to have a minimum tax (counting both income tax and payroll taxes paid by or on behalf of the taxpayer) of, say, 30% at $1 million and, say, 35% at $10 million. The latter tax would hit me much harder and I lean toward it. Just changing the marginal rate would hardly hit me at all.
>
> Let me know your thoughts. Whatever they are, you've still got my vote.
>
> Warren

Clearly, I never wound up running for president. I don't know what would have happened had I tried. I suspect I would have found the whole process profoundly frustrating in the long run. Too often, politics, especially at the national level, is no more than political theater: an endless stage production full of esoteric, conflicting plot lines that lead nowhere. I've seen so many instances where the DC-based political class has tended to operate from an attitude of entitlement, as if the citizenry works to serve them, instead of the other way around. I have already discussed Sen. Elizabeth Warren of Massachusetts and AOC, criticizing their politics along with their discourteousness in not even bothering to respond to reasonable queries and criticisms. But they are by no means the only ones, and neither is their lack of courtesy confined to their own party.

During the summer of 2020, I had occasion to write to Sen. James Inhofe (R–OK) concerning a matter in which I had a particular interest:

July 31, 2020

By Federal Express & Email
The Hon. James M. Inhofe
Chairman, U.S. Senate Armed Services Committee
205 Russell Senate Office Building
Washington, DC 20510
Sarah_Warren@inhofe.senate.gov

Dear Chairman Inhofe:

I write to you because I am concerned that your position on the FCC's approval of Ligado Networks' 5G broadband license is based on specious Department of Defense objections, which fly in the face of overwhelming scientific opinion to the contrary and will only result in our falling further behind the Chinese in deployment of our 5G spectrum.

It has been widely reported that you have placed Mike O'Rielly's nomination for another term as an FCC

Commissioner on hold until he publicly commits to vote to overturn the FCC's current Ligado licensure order approving Ligado's proposal to deploy a low-power mobile broadband network.

"Over the past few months, I have sent letters, held hearings and called countless officials to highlight what we all know to be true (emphasis added): the FCC's Ligado Order is flawed and will lead to significant harm to our military and the thousands of individuals and businesses that rely on GPS," Inhofe said in his Tuesday statement. "I am holding Commissioner O'Rielly's nomination until he publicly states that he will vote to overturn the current Ligado Order. I understand that O'Rielly has stated that he would give 'due consideration to a stay' 'based on new data or evidence' — but that isn't enough. This isn't just about our military, but all users of GPS are united in opposition. All of America can't be wrong, and he understands that. I need his commitment in plain English to vote to overturn the order, not just consider it, before I will allow his nomination to proceed."

In what sense is this something that "we all know to be true?" The FCC's Ligado licensure order was passed by a 5-0 bipartisan vote after five years of extensive analysis by Chairman Ajit Pai and his staff, based on substantial scientific evidence and on impact studies from all interested constituencies. They did their homework before acting. On what basis is your own position predicated?

I know that the FCC's approval is opposed by the Pentagon, several government agencies, airlines and some contractors on the ground that the L-band spectrum that Ligado proposes to use, which is also used by GPS systems, may allegedly cause interference rendering those GPS units used by the military, aircraft and individuals to lose their lock on the satellites. But the weight of scientific evidence, painstakingly reviewed by the FCC, stands against them.

On June 18, 2020, Valerie Green, Ligado's EVP and Chief Legal Officer, wrote to Chairmen Wicker and Pallone of the Senate Committee on Commerce, Science and Transportation and the House Committee on Energy and Commerce, respectively, and to Ranking Members Cantwell and Walden of those two Committees, laying out the history of the FCC's Ligado licensure approval. I am attaching Ms. Green's letter here for your review. In it, she wrote, in part:

> At a hearing before the Senate Commerce Committee earlier this week, Commissioner Mike O'Rielly said in response to a question from Chairman Wicker that NTIA not long ago had a different view on Ligado's FCC application than the one it has recently expressed. Commissioner O'Rielly indicated that the NTIA's current position is inconsistent with the one reached and

held by the engineers and experts at NTIA prior to changes in political personnel there. We at Ligado have known this to be true for some time based on our direct discussions with the NTIA about our application. What is not well understood is that the Department of Defense's Chief Information Office (DoD-CIO) also concluded that Ligado's spectrum plan did not present any harm to GPS devices, and indeed had shared this view with the NTIA and the Federal Communications Commission, and signaled that the experts at NTIA, DoD-CIO and the FCC were on the same page: Ligado's spectrum plan did not present harm to GPS devices.

The FCC's 72-page Ligado Order methodically analyzed the record, including all the evidence and arguments put forth by DoT and NTIA and other stakeholders, and concluded that the proposed spectrum plan was in the public interest and would not harm GPS devices. Though some at DoD now profess surprise at this decision, the attached documents make clear that the spectrum experts at DoD CIO and NTIA had long ago concluded that the testing, the science, and the law dictate that result.

If you are seeing probative scientific evidence that runs counter to what Chairman Pai, the FCC Commissioners and their staff evaluated, and that Ms. Green cites, please adduce it. As Mr. Justice Brandeis famously quipped, "Sunlight is said to be the best of disinfectants." Otherwise, the country will be left to wonder why what was (and should be) a fact-and-science-based decision, reached by a bipartisan panel after five years of scrupulous analysis and consideration, is now being politicized by a Senate Committee that doesn't even have jurisdiction over this matter (highlighted by unseemly, coercive threats to other government officials who disagree with you), to the ultimate detriment of the American people.

At 78, I am old enough to remember President Eisenhower's admonishment, in his 1961 farewell address to the nation, that:

> In the councils of government, we must guard against the acquisition of unwarranted influence, whether sought or unsought, by the military/industrial complex. The potential for the disastrous rise of misplaced power exists and will persist.

I appreciate your reading this letter and look forward to your response.

Sincerely,
Leon G. Cooperman

There was no response to this, nor to a follow-up letter on the same subject. As I write these words, Ligado remains, for the time being, on track to deploy its network in due course, despite significant opposition that remains quite vocal. It will be interesting to see what happens.

PART VI

EPILOGUE

CHAPTER 14

SUMMING UP

The purpose of life is to be useful, to be honorable, to be compassionate, to have it make some difference that you have lived and lived well.

— RALPH WALDO EMERSON

My chief reason for writing this book has been to hammer home several key points: the virtues of our wonderful country as a land of freedom and opportunity; the great positive power of free-market capitalism; the shortcomings of many in the political class as regards their failure to appreciate that they exist to serve the people and not the other way around; the value of hard work; the importance of leading by example; and my rationale for my philanthropic efforts.

I am the son of immigrants, as are so many others. The father of Amazon founder Jeff Bezos came here from Cuba. Longtime Chrysler chairman Lee Iacocca's parents hailed from Italy, as did the parents of my old friend Mario Gabelli. Call it the American dream. In no other country in the world is there the potential for such social mobility as we have here. The option is always there to dream, to learn, to build a career, and to achieve. The basic foundational building blocks are available to all, as the example of my starting out in the New York City public schools, and at a public college, readily shows. Like so many others, I do not come from wealth or from Mayflower roots. But also like so many others, I have found success — great success, such as is only possible within a free capitalist system.

According to an October 2022 essay by Andy Kessler in *The Wall Street Journal,* recent polling indicates that "more than half of eighteen- to twenty-four-year-olds in the U.S. have a negative view of capitalism [and] more than half have a positive view of socialism."

I find this mystifying. Time and time again throughout history, socialist and communist countries have collapsed under their own weight, having inevitably become bastions of underachievement, inefficiency, failed central planning, and (most of all) absence of ambition and innovation among their citizens. Untethered from the fundamental tenets of a free-market system, such as free trade driven by individual self-interest, countries typically labor under stubborn and painful inefficiencies that work to the gross disadvantage of their citizens and tend to totalitarianism. Hopefully, my story will cause at least a few young people to consider the quality of life and the freedoms to be had in the United States as compared to, for example, Cuba, North Korea, or the former Soviet Union, and realize that capitalism works.

But nothing is perfect. As I've endeavored to show from my own experience, many in the American governing/political/regulatory class work, at best, simply for themselves rather than for their constituents or the country. I have no idea how to fix this problem, which, because it is rooted in human nature, is not susceptible of any easy solution.

I hope that through my story I have shown the value of hard work of the type most politicians know little. There are few limits to personal achievement that can't be surmounted through an effortful striving for excellence and a willingness to subordinate short-term pleasure for long-term success.

Most questions have answers, and most problems have solutions. You just have to invest the time and effort to find them. Always be agile. Always be learning. Always be adapting. As the adage goes, "Leap, and the net shall appear." But better still, rather than rely on some magical net, do whatever you can to make sure you land on your feet, and to hell with the net.

Always be agile. Always be learning. Always be adapting.

Ignorance may sometimes be bliss — especially at the beginning of an enterprise, when you are excited by a brilliant idea but don't yet fully appreciate the learning curve and sweat equity involved in bringing it to fruition. But it is that very process of learning and effortfulness that make it all worthwhile in the end, transmuting that brilliant idea from mere concept to profitable reality.

Self-made billionaire and entrepreneur Mark Cuban once stated: "It's not money … or connections that make for success, it's the willingness to outwork and outlearn everyone." Legendary advertising man David Ogilvy astutely observed that "men die of boredom, psychological conflict, and disease. They do not die of hard work." And it was the famed architect Frank Lloyd Wright who affirmed that the price of success is "dedication to hard work and an unremitting devotion to the things you want to see happen."

At both Goldman Sachs and Omega, I never asked anyone to put in more effort or hours than I did myself. I always pushed myself and, in that way, led by example. I've never hesitated to roll up my sleeves to accomplish what I've wanted to see happen. I still don't. I'm still actively engaged. I can't quite grasp the notion of complete retirement that so many others can (and more power to them). If one's passion is golf or yachting, so be it. But my passion, even in my advanced years, still involves a lot of diligent toil, and my toil these days is mostly overseeing my philanthropic giving while managing my personal investments to have the most possible wealth available to maximize and service that philanthropy.

F. Scott Fitzgerald said, "There are no second acts in American lives." But I disagree. Wall Street was my first act. Philanthropy is my second act.

I believe everyone should engage in some form of philanthropy, each in proportion to their ability. I've written about my giving not to brag but to hopefully inspire others to do the same. In funding the Cooperman College Scholars program, and through my gifts to various medical, educational, and other institutions and organizations, large and small, I hope to leave a legacy in the way of young people finding success and becoming good citizens, and in the way of hospitals and schools and charitable nonprofits continuing to further the happiness and progress of mankind.

To be able to do so is a true blessing.

THE MORAL CALCULATIONS OF A BILLIONAIRE

By Eli Saslow

After the best year in history to be among the super rich, one of America's 745 billionaires wonders, "What's enough? What's the answer?"

Reprinted by permission of the Washington Post:

The Moral Calculations of a Billionaire

BY ELI SASLOW

The Washington Post, January 30, 2022

BOCA RATON, Fla. — The stock market had been open for only 17 minutes when Leon Cooperman picked up the phone to check how much money he'd made. He dialed a private line to his trading desk in New Jersey, just as he did a dozen times each day.

"Decent start to the morning?" he asked.

"Oh yeah. The market's shaky, but you're up."

"Give me numbers."

"Looks like six, seven million."

"Fine. Thank you. Let's keep holding steady," said Cooperman, 78. He hung up and watched a stock graph on his computer screen as it rose from one minute to the next, charting another good day to be a billionaire in America. Outside the office, he could see his wife leaving to play in her weekly bridge game and a group of golfers strolling past on a private course. He'd chosen to live in Florida for at least 183 days each year in part to benefit from the state's low tax rate for residents, and from 7 a.m. until midnight he was typically seated at the desk in his office, managing the more than $2.5 billion he'd made during a career as an investor and a hedge fund manager.

He'd been earning more than his family could spend since about 1975, and in the decades since then he'd come to see the act of making money less as a personal necessity than as a serious game he could play and win. He invested it, traded it, lent it, gave it away and watched each day as the accounts continued to grow beyond his needs, his wants and sometimes even his own comprehension.

"I don't want to say it's all play money at this point, but what else could I possibly spend it on?" he sometimes wondered. His wife's walk-in closet was already bigger than the South Bronx apartment where he'd grown up. Their Florida home had a custom-built infinity pool, and in five years he'd never once gone in for a swim.

He checked the stock graph on his screen and called his trading desk again.

"Still good? Any news?"

"Very good, yeah. The highfliers are getting killed, but the value stocks are doing great. You're up about 10 million."

The past year had been the best time in history to be one of America's 745 billionaires, whose cumulative wealth has grown by an estimated 70 percent since the beginning of the pandemic even as tens of millions of low-wage workers have lost their jobs or their homes. Together, those 745 billionaires are now worth more than the bottom 60 percent of American households combined, and each day Cooperman could see that gap widening on his balance sheet — up an average of $4,788 per minute in the stock market, $1.9 million per day and $700 million total in 2021. As a record amount of wealth continued to shift toward a tiny fraction of people at the pinnacle of the economy, Cooperman could sense something else shifting, too.

"Billionaires shouldn't even exist in America," read one note he'd received after he went on TV to recommend stock picks.

"One day, we're coming after all of you with pitchforks," read another message.

"Wake up, moron. YOU and your insatiable greed are at the root of our biggest societal problems."

He responded to most of the personal emails, kept record of the occasional death threats and wrote letters to politicians such as Sen. Elizabeth Warren (D-Mass.), Sen. Bernie Sanders (I-Vt.) and Rep. Alexandria Ocasio-Cortez (D-N.Y.) whenever they criticized billionaires in their speeches, because he couldn't understand: What exactly had he done wrong? What rule had he broken? He'd been born to poor immigrant parents on the losing end of a capitalist economy. He'd attended public schools, taken on debt to become the first in his family to attend college, worked 80-hour weeks, made smart decisions, benefited from some good luck, amassed a fortune for himself and for his clients and paid hundreds of millions in taxes to the government. He had a wife of 57 years, two successful children, and three grandchildren who were helping him decide how to give most of his money away to a long list of charities. "My life is the story of the American Dream," he'd said while accepting an award at one charity gala, and he'd always imagined himself as the rags-to-riches hero, only to now find himself cast as the greedy villain in a story of economic inequality run amok.

And now came another series of emails from a stranger who ran a charity in New Jersey. She said billionaires were avoiding paying their fair share of taxes by using loopholes in the tax code. She said their legacy of excessive wealth was "burdening future generations." She said Cooperman had no idea what it was like to live in poverty or to choose each month between paying rent or buying food.

"She makes decent points," Cooperman said as he read the email again, and it made him think back to a question he'd begun wondering about himself: In a time of historic inequality, what were the moral responsibilities of a billionaire?

"Thank you for your emails. It might be helpful for me to provide you with some background about myself," he wrote back, and then he attached a short biography and copies of his letters to politicians. "There seems to be a fundamental misunderstanding of who I am."

He knew what people imagined when they thought of a billionaire. He'd read the stories of excess and extravagance and witnessed some of it firsthand, but that wasn't him. He didn't spend $238 million on a New York penthouse like hedge fund manager Ken Griffin; or vacation at his own private island in Belize like Bill Gates; or throw himself $10 million birthday parties featuring camels and acrobats like investor Stephen Schwarzman; or drop $70,000 a year on hair care like Donald Trump; or buy a preserved 14-foot shark for an estimated $8 million like Steven Cohen; or spend more than $1 billion on art like media mogul David Geffen; or budget $23 million for personal security like Facebook did for Mark Zuckerberg.

He didn't have his own spaceships like Elon Musk and Jeff Bezos; or a 600-foot flying airship like Sergey Brin; or a decommissioned Soviet fighter jet like Larry Ellison; or a $215 million yacht with a helipad and a pool like Steve Wynn; or a private train with three staterooms like John Paul DeJoria; or a $5 million luxury car collection like Kylie Jenner.

What Cooperman had for transportation was a 25-year-old Schwinn bicycle he liked to ride around the neighborhood and a Hyundai he used for running errands a few times each week.

He rechecked the stock graph on his screen and picked up his phone to call his wife, Toby, who was sitting in her office suite down the hall.

"I'm going to head out and grab some of those Costco lamb chops later," he told her.

"We need anything else?" she asked.

"I don't think so," he said. "I'll just see what's on special."

They'd been together since they met at Hunter College in 1962, when tuition at the public New York university cost as little as $24 per semester and the promise of a life in America was that each generation would surpass the one before. She was the daughter of a struggling pillowcase salesman from Romania; he was the son of a plumber's apprentice who emigrated from Poland at age 13, never finished high school, worked six days a week and later died of a heart attack while carrying a sink up the stairs to a fourth-story apartment.

His father left behind an estate worth less than $100,000, but Cooperman also inherited his father's belief that the economic ladder between poor and rich was short enough to climb with determination and hard work. More than 90 percent of children born in the United States during the 1940s would go on to out-earn their parents; two-thirds of those born into poverty would rise into at least the middle class. Cooperman waited tables during the summers, worked for Xerox while he went to business school at night and then started as an analyst at Goldman Sachs making $12,500 a year. "My PhD is for poor, hungry and driven," he liked to say. He told colleagues that capitalism was like a battle for survival in the African safari and that the key to success was to adopt the mind-set of a lion or a gazelle during a hunt. "When the sun comes up, you'd better be running," Cooperman told them. Within nine years, he'd been named a partner. Within a decade, he was a millionaire.

Together, he and Toby had learned how to be rich, which mostly meant deciding how not to spend their money. He still felt most comfortable shopping for clothes wholesale and commuting to work on New Jersey public transit. Toby enjoyed her job as a special-education teacher even if she didn't need the $25 an hour, so she continued working and donated her salary back to the school. They bought a house for $325,000 in New Jersey in the 1980s and later built their $5 million home in Florida. They worried about demotivating their two children by giving them a massive inheritance, so instead they put a small fraction of their wealth into a trust that could be accessed only once their sons turned 35, at which point one was already a successful businessman and the other was an environmental scientist with a PhD.

Cooperman eventually left Goldman Sachs to start his own hedge fund, Omega, and for two decades he compounded his millions at an average of 14 percent each year as the stock market soared, until he and Toby were among the wealthiest few hundred billionaires in the United States. They were invited to dinner in 2010 by Gates and Warren Buffett, who had just started a program called the Giving Pledge, asking billionaires to donate at least half of their money to charity, and the Coopermans committed that night.

"I could buy a Picasso for a hundred million, but it doesn't turn me on, so then what?" Cooperman told them. "We live a very rational lifestyle. What better use is there for our money?"

They'd given away $150 million to a hospital in New Jersey, $50 million for college scholarships to Newark high school students, $40 million to Columbia Business School, $40 million to Hunter College, $30 million to performing arts, $25 million to the Jewish Family Fund, $20 million to skilled nursing, $15 million to food banks, and on and on it went. But no matter how much they gave away, their money continued to make more money even as wages for the middle class remained essentially flat. In the past 50 years, the gap between poor families and the top 0.1 percent had increased more than tenfold. Children now had only a 43 percent chance of out-earning their parents.

"Mr. Cooperman, your donation is needed to keep the American Dream off life support," read one of the dozens of solicitations he received each day.

"Mr. Cooperman, more than 11 million American children are now living in poverty ..."

"Mr. Cooperman, please help us provide clean drinking water ..."

"Mr. Cooperman, the pandemic has left 60 million families at risk of losing their homes ..."

He donated to more than 50 organizations each year and also to a number of people who wrote to him in personal distress. "Other than my family, writing checks is the most meaningful thing I do," Cooperman said, and yet no matter how many zeros he included, it left him wanting to do more. "We're going in the wrong direction in this country in so many depressing ways," he said. He believed in the meritocratic ideal of capitalism — "equal opportunity if not equal results," he said — but it seemed to him that the odds of success remained stacked by race, by gender and increasingly by economic starting position. Rates of intergenerational poverty had gone up in each of the past three decades. The most disadvantaged children were falling further behind. He believed from his own experience that a college education was the best answer, and yet tuition costs were continuing to skyrocket.

"It's not exactly a fair system until you even up the odds," he said, and after looking over the list of worthy causes, he and Toby had decided that donating half of their money didn't feel sufficient. Sixty percent wasn't enough to meet the country's needs. Neither was 75. So they'd agreed to set up a family foundation that would eventually give away more than 90 percent of their money, and Cooperman had decided that rather than retiring in earnest, he would continue to manage their account so there would be more to give away.

"He who dies rich dies disgraced," read a quotation attributed to Andrew Carnegie on Cooperman's office desk, but on this day he was still rich and getting richer. "What's enough?" he wondered. "What's the answer?" He checked the stock graph on his screen — up $2.6 million in the past five hours. His accounts were equal to the average net worth of 23,000 middle-class American families.

Each day when the stock market closed at 4 p.m., he checked the final numbers on his 40 stock holdings, reviewed his investment strategy for the next day and then left for a two-mile walk around the palm trees and putting greens of St. Andrews Country Club in Boca Raton. The community was set off from the surrounding suburbs by a canal, a gatehouse, a 10-foot wall and an infrared security system. A few of the 700 homes were owned by other billionaires, and most others belonged to millionaires who wintered in Florida. All of the residents had gotten richer during the pandemic as the luxury real estate market exploded and their home values surged by more than 40 percent.

Cooperman walked past an old designer home that was being torn down and rebuilt into a new designer home. He continued up the road toward the clay tennis courts, the spa and the terraced clubhouse. A resident drove by in a new Bentley, and Cooperman waved and then watched the $200,000 car drive on. "You get a lot of people who show off their wealth," he said, "but I could buy and sell that guy 100 times."

He and Toby had spent almost all of their time during the pandemic within the gates of St. Andrews, eating dinner outside at the clubhouse and playing cards with friends, but every few days they liked to go for a drive. Once, early in the pandemic, they'd driven to a quiet, nearby park only to find more than 150 cars lined up in the parking lot as people waited for bags of canned goods at an impromptu food bank.

"Depressing and staggering in a country of such wealth," Cooperman said, and it made him remember a poem his granddaughter had written and published when she was in middle school, called "Seven Miles," about the physical proximity between the extreme wealth of Short Hills, N.J., where Cooperman had his other home, and the extreme poverty in nearby Newark. "At one end we have too much," she'd written. "At the other, they have nothing. Spread it all just seven miles."

She'd gone on to graduate Phi Beta Kappa from Stanford, becoming an "ultraliberal, socialist type in favor of wealth redistribution," Cooperman said. He adored her and admired both her empathy and her intellect, but he'd repeatedly fought against the liberal idea that one way to redistribute that wealth was to tax billionaires at a rate of 70 percent or more. He'd written to Sen. Warren about her "soak-the-rich positions," and to President Barack Obama about "villainizing success." He was a registered independent, and he'd voted for Joe Biden in the last election because he considered President Donald Trump a "would-be dictator whose comportment in office was beyond disgraceful," but Cooperman believed most of all in the basic tenets of capitalism. He'd earned his money, and therefore it was his to spend or give away. He sent in a quarterly check for $10 million to the federal government in estimated taxes and said he paid an effective tax rate of 34 percent. He'd told politicians in his letters that he was willing to pay more, but he believed the highest effective tax rate should be no more than 50 percent.

"What made America great is our system of capitalism, incentivizing work and effort and ingenuity," he'd written. "Capitalism has flaws, but socialism has no benefits. Why not spread my work ethic instead of just my wealth?"

Now he looped around a cul-de-sac and turned back toward his house. For years, he'd been doing these daily walks with his brother, Howard, until he died in December at age 85, and lately Cooperman had been thinking back over their lives. Cooperman had chosen to wake up at 5:15 each morning and devote 80 hours every week to his work, taking off only the Friday after Thanksgiving. His brother, meanwhile, had chosen not to go to college and then retired as soon as he could. He preferred to play racquetball, go to the casino with friends and volunteer as a wheelchair transporter at the hospital. Cooperman had ended up with his billions and his name on top of the hospital entrance; his brother had died with relatively modest amounts of money but with a cellphone loaded with numbers for dozens of close friends.

"We both got what we worked for," Cooperman said. "We were best friends, and we admired what each other had, but it would have been wrong to take what I earned and given it all over to him."

He walked up his circular driveway, into the house and back toward his office.

"Different choices, different outcomes," he said. "The world isn't meant to be totally even."

His choice: 12 more hours anchored to the chair in his office, monitoring the market and calling in to his trading desk again and again as the sun reflected off the swimming pool outside his window. The market fell. The market rose. He bought $3 million in distressed bonds. He gave another $5 million away to charity. He was $18 million up for the day. He was $6 million down. He was beating the market again by mid-morning, losing at lunch, winning an hour later, and then losing again. "Does it make any sense?" he asked himself, watching the numbers change on his screen. "To sit inside all day in front of a machine, making money I don't need so I can give it to someone I don't know?"

He'd been wondering since his brother's death whether there were better ways to spend some of his time, so one afternoon before the stock market closed, he shut off his computer and drove a few miles outside the gates of St. Andrews to visit Florida Atlantic University. The school's president had invited Cooperman to speak to a group of low-income college students about his career and his values.

"Believe it or not, I have a great deal of commonality with all of you," Cooperman said as he stood at the lectern and looked out at the crowd of about 40 students from a university scholarship program much like the one Cooperman and his wife had started in New Jersey. Most were students of color who had been born to immigrant parents. All of them came from families with incomes of $30,000 or less. The students had been living on campus during the pandemic as some of their families were upended by layoffs, by evictions, by a Haitian earthquake, by a Dominican drought, by coronavirus infections and covid-19 deaths.

"I can understand some of the challenges you're facing right now," Cooperman said, starting a short PowerPoint presentation about his journey from a one-bedroom apartment to the Forbes 400 list of wealthiest Americans.

"I worked very hard. I wanted to win," he told them as he flipped to the next slide.

"I'm a great believer in capitalism," he said. "We have the best economic system in the world."

"How do you become wealthy?" he asked. "You develop a product or a service that people want. The world is better off for a Larry Ellison, a Bill Gates. Look at the jobs they created. Look at the good they did for the world. The attack on wealthy people makes no sense to me."

"I'm giving the money away," he said. "It's been my pledge, and my wife's pledge, to give it all away."

He finished going through the slides and then asked for questions, and after a while a student in the center of the room raised her hand and waited for the microphone. She said she was also interested in a career in business, and she explained that one of the many barriers in her way was the start-up cost. "In Florida, you need $200," she said.

"You're going to need a lot more than that," Cooperman said.

"I know," she said. "I just mean two hundred to get the license, the paperwork, from zero."

Cooperman looked at her for a moment and tried to imagine what it would mean to start again from zero, and what it would be like to ascend from poverty to extreme wealth not in the 1960s but in 2022, when that gap had multiplied 10 times. But he'd occupied these students' place in the American economy once. His faith in the American Dream required him to believe that they could one day occupy his.

"I'll admit, it's very hard," he said. "It's gotten harder. But the 99 percent can still join the 1 percent. It's possible with enough luck and commitment."

He told them about how he'd gotten up each morning at 5:15; how he'd chosen a job that he loved; how he'd gotten his PhD in being poor, hungry and driven; how he'd followed his instincts; how he'd attacked each day like a lion chasing a gazelle as he raced to the pinnacle of the economy and the 99 percent receded behind him.

"I can speak to the issues of both being rich and being poor," he told them, and as a billionaire in the bifurcating American economy, there was one truth of which he felt certain.

"Being rich is better," he said.

Eli Saslow is a reporter at The Washington Post. He won the 2014 Pulitzer Prize for Explanatory Reporting for his year-long series about food stamps in America. He was also a finalist for the Pulitzer Prize in Feature Writing in 2013, 2016 and 2017.

Printed in the USA
CPSIA information can be obtained
at www.ICGtesting.com
LVHW071936170923
758456LV00033B/1160/J